ARTBOOKS

FROM CRESCENT MOON
PUBLISHING

Leonardo da Vinci
by James Pearson

Early Netherlandish Painting
by Rosalind Mutter

Memling
By W.H.J. & J.C. Weale

Van Eyck
By J. Cyril M. Weale

Piero della Francesca
by Naomi Haskell

Giovanni Bellini
by Julia Davis

Eric Gill: Nuptials of God
by Anthony Hoyland

*Minimal Art and Artists In the
1960s and After*
by Laura Garrard

*Vincent van Gogh: Visionary
Landscapes*
by Stuart Morris

*Mark Rothko: The Art of
Transcendence*
by Julia Davis

Jasper Johns
by L.M. Poole

Brice Marden
by Laura Garrard

*Frank Stella: American Abstract
Artist*
by James Pearson

*Maurice Sendak and the Art of
Children's Book Illustration*
by L.M. Poole

*Sex in Art: Pornography and
Pleasure in Painting and
Sculpture*
by Cassidy Hughes

The Art of Andy Goldsworthy
by William Malpas

*Andy Goldsworthy: Touching
Nature*
by William Malpas

Andy Goldsworthy In Close-Up
by William Malpas

Andy Goldsworthy In America
by William Malpas

Andy Goldsworthy: Pocket Guide
by William Malpas

The Art of Richard Long
by William Malpas

Richard Long: Pocket Guide
by William Malpas

*Constantin Brancusi: Sculpting the
Essence of Things*
by James Pearson

*Alison Wilding: The Embrace of
Sculpture*
by Susan Quinnell

Erotic Art In the 19th Century
By Cassidy Hughes

Erotic Art In the Renaissance
By Cassidy Hughes

Erotic Art
By Cassidy Hughes

The Erotic Object: Sexuality in Sculpture From Prehistory to the Present Day
by Susan Quinnell

Land Art: A Complete Guide
by William Malpas

Land Art In Close-Up
by William Malpas

Land Art In Great Britain
by William Malpas

Land Art In the U.S.A.
by William Malpas

Installation Art In Close-Up
by William Malpas

Colorfield Painting
by Laura Garrard

Bellini
By James Mason

Botticelli
By Henry Binns

Renaissance In Italy: The Fine Arts
By John Addington Symonds

The Life of Michelangelo Buonarroti
By John Addington Symonds

Michelangelo Buonarroti
By Charles Holroyd

Michelangelo
By Estelle Hurll

Michelangelo
By Romain Rolland

Correggio
By Estelle M. Hurll

Tintoretto
By S.L. Bensusan

Titian: A Collection of Fifteen Pictures
By Estelle M. Hurll

The Earlier Work of Titian
By Claude Phillips

The Later Work of Titian
By Claude Phillips

The Earlier and Later Work of Titian
By Claude Phillips

Bernardino Luini
By James Mason

Perugino
By Selwyn Brinton

Perugino
By George Williamson

Raphael
By Estelle M. Hurll

Raphael
By Paul Konody

Dante Gabriel Rossetti
By Esther Wood

Recollections of Dante Gabriel Rossetti
By T. Hall Caine

Burne-Jones
By A. Lys Baldry

The Whistler Book
By Sadakichi Hartmann

Whistler
By T. Martin Wood

Rodin: The Man and His Art
Edited by Judith Cladel

Rodin
By Rainer Maria Rilke

Auguste Rodin
By Camille Mauclair

Corot
By Sidney Allnutt

Fra Angelico
By Jennie Ellis Keysor

Fra Angelico
By James Mason

Fra Angelico
By J.B. Supino

Aubrey Beardsley
By Robert Ross

The Art of Aubrey Beardsley
By Arthur Symons

Leighton
By Ernest Rhys

Millais
By A. Lys Baldry

The Madonna In Art
By Estelle Hurll

Women In the Fine Arts
By Clara Erskine Clement

The Venetian School of Painting
By Evelyn Phillipps

Boucher
By Haldane McFall

Fragonard
By Haldane McFall

Leonardo da Vinci
By Maurice Brockwell

Famous European Painters
By Sarah Bolton

Great Artists
By Jennie Ellis Keysor

Great Pictures
Edited by Esther Singleton

Knights of Art
By Amy Steedman

Delacroix
By Paul Konody

Ingres
By A.J. Finberg

Goya
By Francis Crastre

Dürer
By Hertbert Furst

Albrecht Dürer
By T. Sturge Moore

Dürer
By M.F. Sweetser

Rembrandt van Rijn
By Malcolm Bell

Rembrandt and His Works
By John Burnet

Rembrandt and His Etchings
By Louis Holman

Rembrandt
By Estelle M. Hurll

Rembrandt
By Josef Israels

Turner
By C. Lewis Hind

Turner
By W. Cosmo Monkhouse

The Art of Katsuhiro Otomo
By Jeremy Robinson

The Art of Masamune Shirow
By Jeremy Robinson

MANTEGNA

MANTEGNA

NANCY BELL

CRESCENT MOON

First published 1911. This edition © 2024.

Set in Book Antiqua 10 on 14pt.
Designed by Radiance Graphics.

British Library Cataloguing in Publication data

ISBN-13 9781861716583
ISBN-13 9781861710771

CRESCENT MOON PUBLISHING
P.O. Box 1312, Maidstone, Kent, ME14 5XU
Great Britain, www.crmoon.com

CONTENTS

NOTE ON THE TEXT

The text is from *Mantegna* by Nancy Bell (Mrs Arthur Bell), and published by T.C. & E.C. Jack, London, 1911.

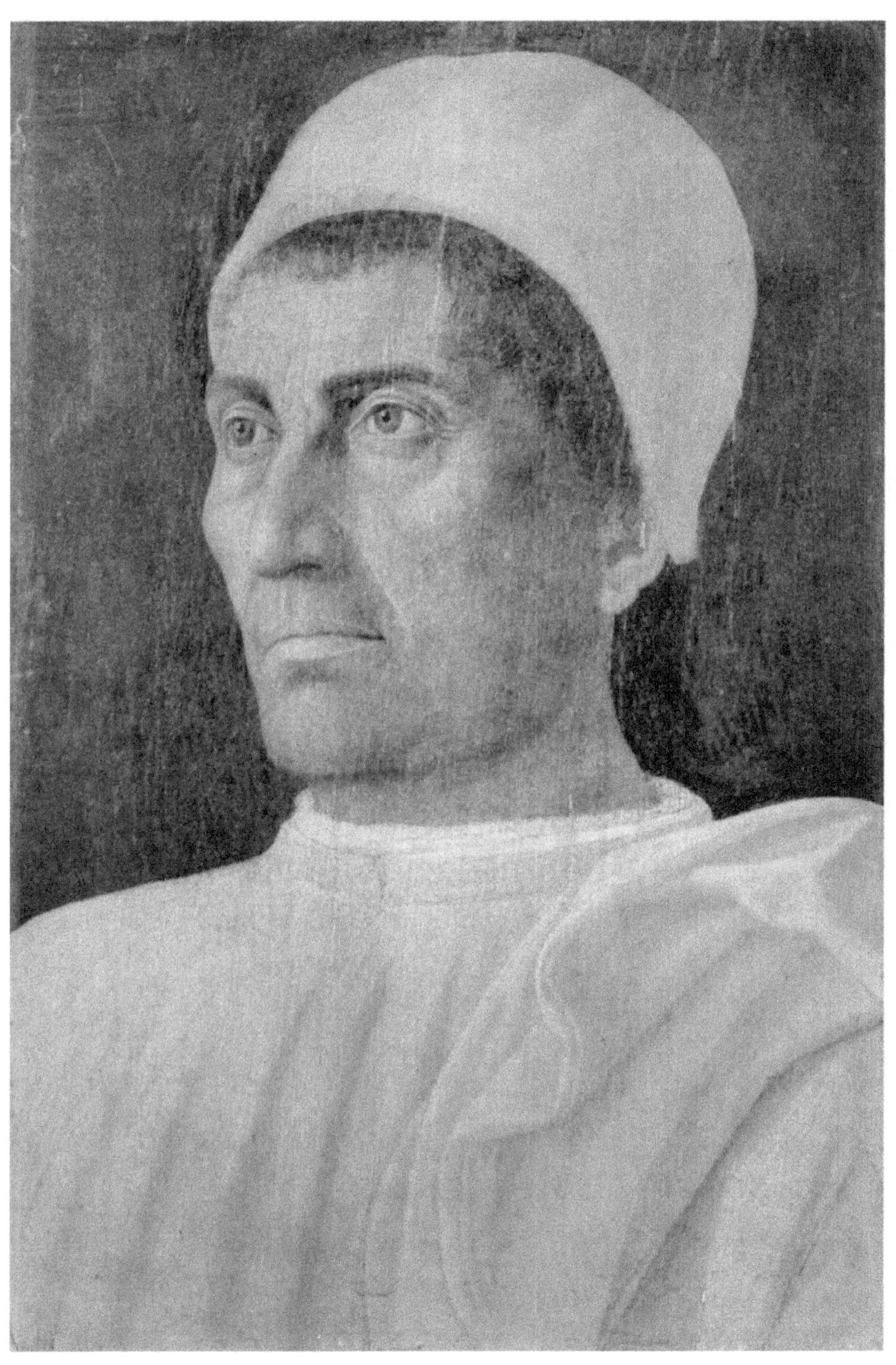

Andrea Mantegna, Portrait of Carlo de' Medici, Uffizi Gallery

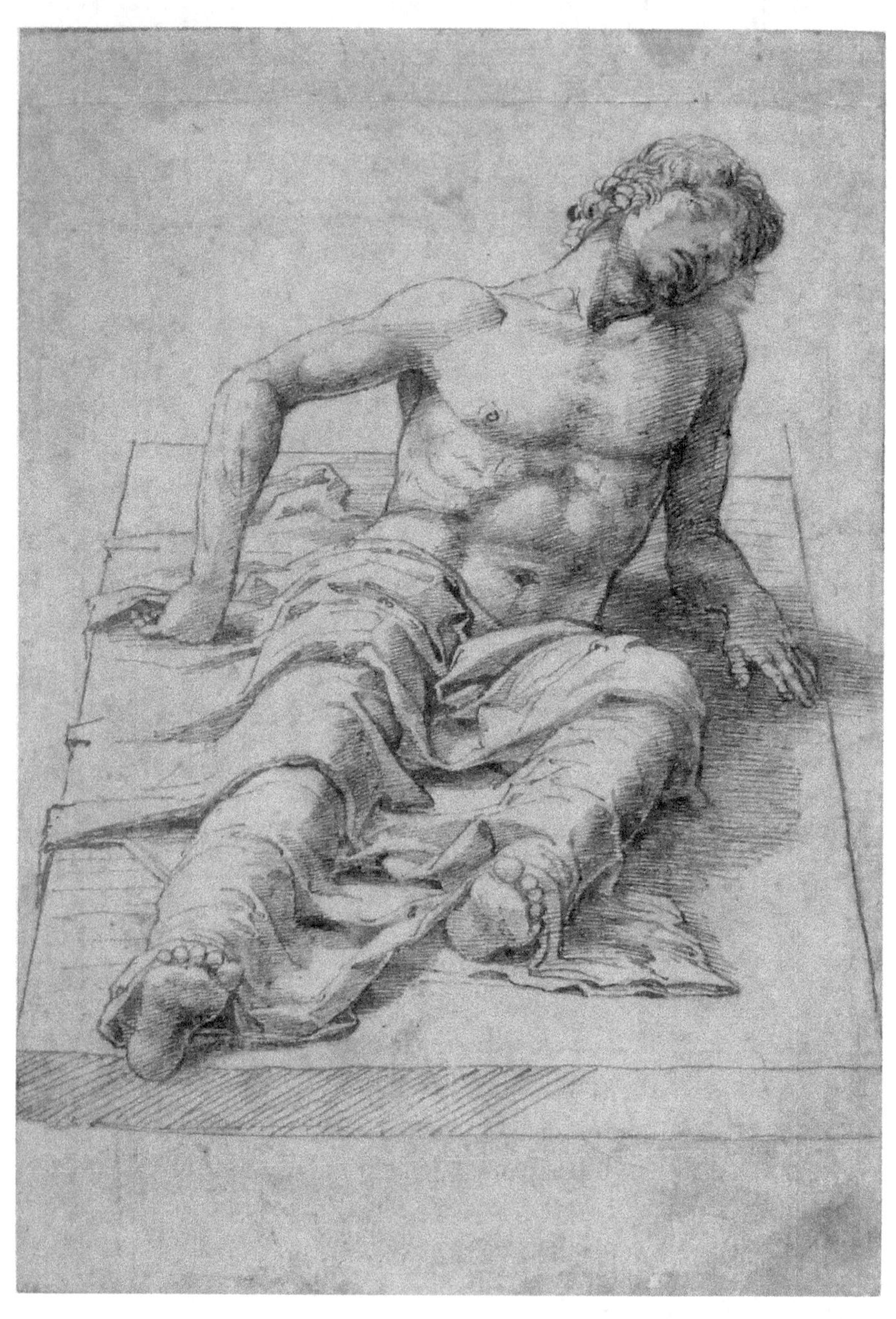

Andrea Mantegna, Man On the Ground, 1510-11, British Museum

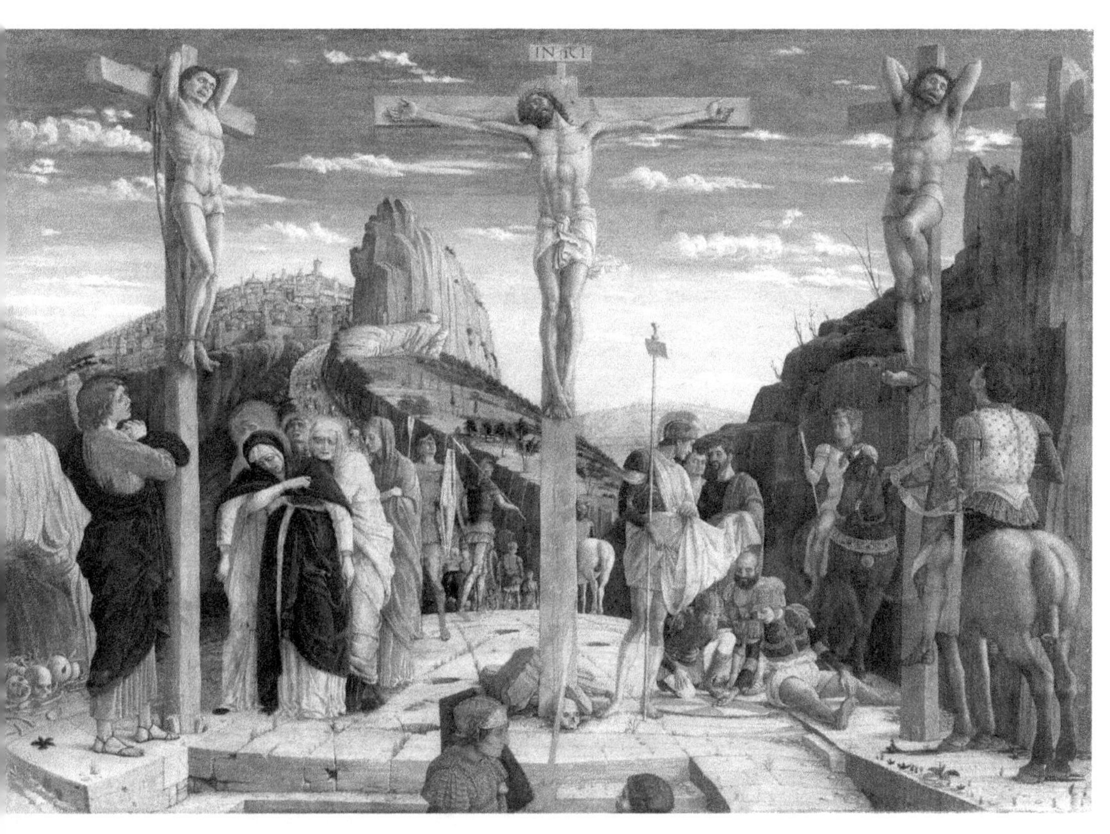

Andrea Mantegna, Predella, San Zen Altarpiece, Verona, 1457, Louvre

Born at a time of exceptional intellectual and æsthetic activity, when Italian humanism was nearing its fullest development, and the art of painting, after a protracted struggle with mechanical difficulties, had at last obtained an almost complete mastery over its media, with a real grasp of the long-neglected science of perspective, Andrea Mantegna may justly be said to have been a true representative of the early Renaissance in Italy, an earnest combatant in the arduous struggle for liberty of thought and expression in which so many of his gifted fellow-countrymen were engaged. A true kindred spirit of his greater contemporary, Donatello, with whom he was in closer rapport than with any painter, the chief characteristic of his work being the plastic rather than the pictorial treatment of form, he was, like him, imbued from the first with a reverent love of truth and a conscientious desire faithfully to interpret it. Mantegna has, indeed, been sometimes charged with a too close imitation of the famous sculptor, but this is manifestly unfair, for, although there can be no doubt that he owed much to Donatello, who was the first to lead him into the right path, by showing him how Nature should be studied, the secret of the strong resemblance between the styles of the two masters is that both went to the same source for inspiration: the best existing examples of antique sculpture, which appeared to them the noblest extant expression of the ideal in the real.

According to some authorities, Vicenza was the birthplace of Mantegna, whilst others claim that honour for Padua; but all agree in stating that he was born in 1431. Of his parents scarcely anything is known, but it is generally supposed that they died at Padua when Andrea was still quite a child, and it is certain that the orphan boy was adopted at once by the artist Francesco

Squarcione, who received him into his own home and began his art education. The true relations between him and his foster-father are, however, very obscure, critics differing greatly with regard to them; but it is very evident that the tastes and ambitions of the two artists were never in real accord, though gratitude for kindness received when he was left alone in the world, long restrained Mantegna from an open breach with the protector of his childhood. The probability is that Squarcione, whose work, judging from the few specimens that have been preserved, was of a very mediocre character, was merely the nominal head of a bottega, or studio, in which painters of far greater eminence than himself, including Jacopo Bellini, were visiting masters. However that may have been, it is certain that several hundred students were at different times under his roof, and, whether they did or did not learn much from him, they had the advantage of seeing the drawings after the antique that he had brought back with him from the trips he delighted in taking to Greece and the Italian towns, that owned collections of classic sculpture.

That Andrea early showed remarkable talent is proved by his having been made, when he was but ten years old, a member of the Guild of Paduan Artists, to which belonged all the leading painters, sculptors, and craftsmen of the city, and association with them must have done much to aid his art-development. He was, indeed, from the very first surrounded by inspiring influences, for Padua, with its noble University, founded in 1222, had long been a leader in antiquarian research, and was already beginning to rival even Florence and Venice as a centre of literary and artistic activity. The quaint mediæval Palace, with its magnificent fifteenth-century roof, the fine Basilica of S. Antonio and the Cappella di S. Giorgio both adorned with the frescoes of Altichiero and Alvanzo, and, above all, the Cappella di Sta. Maria dell' Arena, enriched with the wonderful creations of Giotto, must have been to the enthusiastic young painter a source of continual delight as well as a spur to emulation; although as yet Donatello, destined to give to him the final impulse in the right direction, had not come to Padua to put in hand the glorious bas-reliefs of the high altar of S. Antonio, and the even more remarkable bronze equestrian statue of Gattamelata, that was to inaugurate a new departure in modern realistic sculpture.

Of the first meeting between the veteran sculptor, who, on his arrival in Padua in 1443, was in his fifty-eighth year, and the youthful painter there is no record; but there is no doubt that the latter was privileged to watch the growth of the S. Antonio sculptures, and to listen to the discussions concerning them and their author that took place amongst the masters and students in the bottega of Squarcione. From his first appearance on the scene Donatello dominated the art world of the University city, his personality as well as his work everywhere arousing the greatest enthusiasm. So overwhelming indeed were the attentions heaped upon him that he resisted all invitations to remain after he had completed the work he had actually promised to do, and, even before his monumental piece of sculpture was set up, he fled from the atmosphere of adulation in which he lived back to his native Florence, where, to quote his own words, he "got censured continually." He was still, however, at Padua when, in 1446, Mantegna completed his first independent commission, a "Madonna in Glory" for S. Sofia, now lost, but which is said to have been a wonderful production for a boy still in his teens, clearly betraying the influence both of Donatello and Jacopo Bellini, yet with a marked individuality of its own.

The "Madonna in Glory" is supposed to have been succeeded by other compositions of a similar kind; but the earliest signed work from Andrea's hand is a fresco, dated 1452, above the central door of S. Antonio, representing Saints Antony and Bernardino holding up a wreath bearing the monogram of Christ. In it, as well as in the polyptych of "St. Luke," now in the Brera Gallery, Milan, – that betrays a slight affinity with the Vivarini, – the "Presentation in the Temple," of the Berlin Museum, and the "Adoration of the Magi," in the collection of Lady Ashburton – all painted between 1452 and 1455 – are already noticeable the naturalistic treatment of form, plasticity of modelling, and sombre colouring, that were from first to last characteristic of Mantegna, with a suggestion of the dignified restraint and solemn rhythm of movement, which were later further to distinguish his style. It is, moreover, noticeable that in the two last named, as well as in other early representations of the Virgin and the Holy Child, such as that in the Poldi-Pezzoli Museum, Milan, it is the purely human relationship between the loving mother and her helpless little one which is most forcibly brought out, there being absolutely no suggestion of the supernatural. In the "Presentation in the Temple" Mary clings to the Babe as if unwilling to let Him leave her arms for a moment, and in the "Adoration" her face expresses a tender yearning that is infinitely touching; whereas in later Holy Families from the same hand the Infant Jesus becomes ever more and more aloof and dignified, until at last He appears like a young God conscious of His power to save and bless, whilst His mother withdraws into the background.

More important, perhaps, from a technical point of view, than these independent oil-paintings are the series of frescoes in the Eremitani Chapel, in which can be clearly traced the gradual development of Mantegna's style. In them he for the first time proved himself able successfully to carry out a vast and elaborate scheme of decoration, each composition with its appropriate setting, though complete in itself, contributing to the general effect of the whole. Exactly when the great undertaking was begun is not known, but it is supposed that the commission for it was given to Squarcione about 1452, and its execution entrusted by him to Mantegna, who in 1448 had signed an agreement binding him to the service of his foster-father for a long term of years. In a will dated January 5, 1443, the Chapel of the Eremitani was bequeathed by its then owner, Antonio degli Ovetari, to Jacopo Leone, on condition that after the testator's death seven hundred golden ducats should be expended on its decoration with scenes from the lives of Saints James and Christopher. The subjects, and possibly also the positions they were to occupy, were thus determined beforehand; and it is evident from internal evidence that not all the frescoes are from Mantegna's own hand, but his spirit dominates them all, and those for which he is entirely responsible, especially the "St. James led to Execution," the "Martyrdom" and the "Burial of St. Christopher," mark a great advance, alike in design and in technical execution, on anything hitherto produced by their author. In the first, Mantegna approached more nearly to Donatello in the expression of movement than he had previously done, and displayed very great skill in concentrating the attention upon the figure of the martyr, who pauses to bless and heal a lame man kneeling at his feet, the soldiers halting to look on, and the spectators turning back to see what delays the procession. The "Martyrdom" and "Burial of St. Christopher" are also strikingly dramatic, giving very vivid presentments of the final scenes in the long-protracted agony of the twice-martyred victim, who was found to be still living after he was supposed to have been shot to death; but, unfortunately, both compositions are so much defaced that it is difficult to form a true idea of what they originally were.

The years during which Mantegna was at work on the Eremitani frescoes, supposed to have been completed in 1455, coincided with the most interesting period of the artist's life from a personal point of view. In 1453 he became engaged to the only daughter of Jacopo Bellini, Nicolasia, whom he had known since she was a child, and to whom he had long been attached. He was married to her in 1455, and the young couple evidently started life together under very happy auspices; but little is really known either of their courtship or their later experiences. Neither, unfortunately, is it possible to call up with any semblance of reality the personality of the bride, for although she certainly often posed for her father, husband, and brothers, her portrait cannot be identified in any of their compositions. That she was beautiful and charming is generally taken for granted, that she shared the æsthetic faculty with which the other members of her family were so richly endowed is more than probable, and that she was a good wife to Mantegna is incidentally proved by the fact that his money difficulties did not begin till after her death; but that is all that can be gathered concerning her. It is far easier to realise what the bridegroom was like, for Andrea has introduced himself among the spectators in the "Martyrdom of St. Christopher" and in the later "Meeting between Lodovico Gonzaga and his son, Cardinal Francesco," of the Camera degli Sposi at Mantua, in both of which the painter appears as a handsome, distinguished-looking man whose somewhat stern features, in which, however, there is no suggestion of the irritable temper with which some of his contemporaries charged him, greatly resemble those of the fine bronze bust, of uncertain authorship, that was set up in 1560 outside his mortuary chapel in S. Andrea, Mantua, by one of his grandsons.

Almost the only comment made by the biographers of Mantegna on his marriage is that after it the influence of Jacopo Bellini over his style became more marked, and nearly all they have to tell concerning him and his wife is that they had three boys, one of whom died in infancy, and two girls. Occasionally, it is true, a reference is made to work done in their father's studio by one or the other of the surviving sons, whose names were Francesco and Lodovico. The marriages of the daughters, Laura and Taddea, are alluded to *en passant*, and the fact is mentioned that in his old age the great painter had a natural son, to whom he gave the names of Giovanni Andrea, and whom he confided on his death-bed to the care of the boy's half-brother Lodovico; but scarcely any details can be gathered concerning the home life of the master before Nicolasia passed away, nor has any one been able to ascertain who was the heroine of the romance of the master's closing years. Even Dr. Paul Kristeller in his monumental work, in which is gathered together from an infinite variety of sources everything that can throw light on the character, aims, and work of Mantegna, is able to do no more than suggest that he and his family were on affectionate terms with each other, that he had the best interests of his children at heart, and that his wife shared the tender poetic sensibility of her gifted brother, Giovanni Bellini.

To make up for the meagreness of intimate personal information with which writers on Mantegna have to contend, they one and all dwell at great length on every incident of his art career, describing minutely, for instance, the strained relations between him and Squarcione, which culminated in 1456 in his bringing an action against the latter. It was decided in favour of Andrea, who pleaded that he had been under age when he signed the agreement already alluded to above, and that the conditions of the arrangement made had been broken by his foster-father. It is further related that Squarcione was from the first bitterly hostile to the intimacy between Mantegna and the Bellini, resenting the influence Jacopo exercised over a pupil he looked upon as his own special protégé. When he heard of the engagement between Andrea and Nicolasia, he vowed he would never consent to the match, and when he found that his sanction of the marriage was dispensed with, his indignation knew no bounds. He vented his annoyance by making unreasonable demands upon Mantegna's time, and by harsh criticism of his work on the Eremitani frescoes, in which he all too clearly betrayed his jealousy of the younger artist's superior talent. There was really nothing left for Mantegna to do but to sever all connection with so unreasonable an employer, but that he did so with regret, remembering past kindnesses, is proved by his having put off the rupture as long as he did. It was well for him when he finally left the Squarcione bottega and became free to work out, unchecked, his own art salvation, and henceforth he may truly be said to have gone on from strength to strength, until at last, in such masterpieces as the "Triumph of Cæsar" and the "Madonna della Vittoria," he reached the very zenith of his powers.

The second period of Mantegna's career begins with the painting of the fine triptych for S. Zeno, Verona, commissioned by the enlightened papal protonotary, Abbot Gregorio Correr, one of the leading ecclesiastics of his time, the first of the many distinguished patrons who now began to seek to secure the services of the young painter of Padua. The altar-piece of S. Zeno, the chief composition of which belongs to the class known as "sacro conversazione," in which saints of different periods are grouped about the Virgin and Child, marks a very considerable advance in the delineation of character. The personalities of men so diverse as Saints Peter, John the Evangelist, Augustine, and Zeno are realised with great success, and the concentration of the light on the figure of the Infant Jesus foreshadows the great change that was ere long to take place in the artist's renderings of the Holy Family. It is much to be regretted that the complete work can no longer be seen as it was when first placed in position, for it was carried off by the French in 1797; and although after the Treaty of Vienna the upper portion was restored to S. Zeno, where it now hangs in the choir, the three subjects of the predella, that are also of great significance in the study of the development of Mantegna's style, remained in France – the "Crucifixion," a noble but terribly realistic conception, occupying a place of honour in the Louvre, whilst the "Agony in the Garden" and the "Ascension," that originally flanked it on either side, are at Tours.

Whilst engaged in his arduous undertaking for Abbot Correr, Mantegna painted three of his few portraits – that, now at Berlin, of Cardinal Luigi Mezzarota, the warlike prelate who led the papal troops against the Turks in 1457, defeating them with great loss; that, in the Naples Museum, of Cardinal Francesco Gonzaga, who received the red hat before he was seventeen; and the famous double likeness of John of Czezomicze, better known as Janus Pannonius, that is unfortunately lost, but won for its author great renown and inspired the beautiful elegy addressed to him by the poet on its completion.

Between Cardinal Francesco and Andrea a very strong friendship was soon formed, which may possibly have had something to do with the pressing invitations Mantegna now began to receive from the father of the young prelate Lodovico, the reigning Marquis of Mantua, who worthily maintained the great traditions of his ancestors, under whose auspices the ancient fortress that was to become so inseparably associated with the memory of the Paduan master was enlarged and strengthened, and the Grand Cathedral with the noble Renaissance Church of S. Andrea were built. The first of Lodovico's invitations was probably a verbal one, but it was quickly succeeded by urgent written appeals, some of which have been preserved, in which the writer offers to make Mantegna his court painter with a high salary and to accord him certain valuable privileges, the letters reflecting not only the high esteem in which painters of eminence were then held and the eagerness with which their work was competed for, but also the great sacrifices that were demanded from them, and were such as no modern art patron would dream of exacting.

Again and again Mantegna put off his final reply to the Marquis, for he loved Padua, where he found plenty of congenial employment, and was surrounded with appreciative friends; but at last he yielded, attracted probably partly by the material advantages of the position offered to him, and partly by the exceptional facilities he would have in Mantua for the antiquarian research in which he delighted. It was in the latter half of 1459 that he arrived, accompanied by Nicolasia and their two little children, in the famous city, where he was eagerly welcomed by the Marquis and his wife, the Marchesa Barbara, and their two sons, Federico and Cardinal Francesco. From that time to his death, except for two years spent in Rome, Mantegna worked almost exclusively for the Gonzaga family, becoming ever more and more devotedly attached to them and their interests. From the first, the position of the court painter appears to have been a very enviable one, for, although it is true that the payment of his salary was sometimes delayed, he was evidently on terms of the closest intimacy with his patron, who soon after his arrival granted him a coat of arms embodying his own device, and, as proved by many a still extant letter, was ever ready to help and advise him, whether in matters so trivial as the cut of a coat or so serious as legal disputes concerning the boundaries of property owned by the artist. That the poverty of which Mantegna sometimes complained must have been purely nominal is indeed evident from these lawsuits, as well as from the fact that he was able to make a very valuable collection of antiquities and to give large dowries to his daughters when they married.

The first pictures painted at Mantua were the beautiful triptych of the "Adoration of the Kings," "Circumcision," and "Ascension," now in the Uffizi, Florence; the "Death of the Virgin," in the Prado Gallery; and the remarkable "Pietà," of the Brera Gallery; the last probably a study only, as it was still in Mantegna's studio when the artist passed away, for which reason it has erroneously been attributed to a later period. Unpleasing though it is with its startling realism, the "Dead Christ" is of special value as a study in perspective, and, in the opinion of Dr. Kristeller, it was painted with a view to its being seen from below, for he says, "It is only as a ceiling painting, with its perspective point of sight coinciding with the central point of the ceiling, that the figure would appear correctly foreshortened. There can be no doubt," he adds, "that it was painted as a preliminary study for the nude youth standing inside the balustrade on the ceiling decoration of the Camera degli Sposi and for other figures in ceiling pictures." However that may be, the strange composition stands alone among its author's works, and will probably always remain a subject of contention to critics, so variously do its peculiarities affect different temperaments.

In addition to the oil-paintings quoted above, Mantegna also produced between 1459 and 1460 a large number of frescoes for the various residences of the Marquis of Mantua, but unfortunately no trace of them remains. The earliest extant works of the kind are those of the Camera degli Sposi in the Castello di Corte, which were completed in 1474, and in spite of their melancholy condition of decay, the result chiefly of their having been executed on a dry instead of a damp surface, are ranked amongst the most noteworthy examples of fifteenth-century decorative art in existence. Not only are they admirably executed and thoroughly suitable for the position they occupy, but they also inaugurate a new departure in historical portraiture, the principal subjects being groups of the various members of the Gonzaga family, the most interesting and characteristic of which is, perhaps, that representing the meeting between the Marquis Lodovico and Cardinal Francesco, already referred to as containing a portrait of the artist.

In the other frescoes of the Camera degli Sposi the Cardinal, who by this time had become Papal Legate of Bologna and Bishop of Mantua, is conspicuous by his absence, his high position in the Church making his visits to his home very rare, and leading to his being received with much pomp and ceremony when he did appear. On this occasion he and his father, who was accompanied by his two eldest grandsons, were each attended by a great retinue, and Mantegna has managed with considerable skill, whilst preserving a certain homeliness, to convey an impression of grandeur, the noble figures of the actors in the scene standing out against a fine landscape background, from which rises up the city of Mantua.

The decorations of the Camera degli Sposi so delighted the Marquis that he presented their author with an estate in the heart of the city, on which Mantegna at once began to build a princely mansion, part of which is now converted into a college. Long before it was finished, however, he was saddened by the death of Lodovico, who passed away in 1478, soon after he had commissioned what was to be his beloved court painter's greatest masterpiece – the series of pictures representing the "Triumph of Cæsar," that are now at Hampton Court, having been bought in 1624 from the then reigning Marquis by Charles I. Lodovico was succeeded by his son Federico, who treated Mantegna with the same affectionate consideration as his predecessor had done, taking a deep interest in his welfare and sympathising with him in his domestic anxieties. On October 25, 1478, he wrote to the artist, who had been unable to complete some work for him through illness, begging him to try and get well as quickly as possible, but not to worry about the delay, and later he did all in his power for Mantegna's delicate boy, inquiring constantly after him, and giving his father a letter of introduction to the famous physician, Girardo da Verona, that is of special interest, affording, as it does, an all-too-rare glimpse of the painter as a man as well as an artist, trembling for the life of his suffering child. The Marquis begs the doctor, to consult whom Mantegna took his son to Venice in 1480, "to show every possible consideration to our noble and well-beloved servant"; and though the journey was all in vain, the patient having died soon after the return to Mantua, the solicitude shown on his behalf by the Marquis must have touched the heart of his sorrowing parents.

In 1481 the court of Mantua was thrown into mourning by the death of the Dowager-Marchesa Barbara, who had from the first been a very kind friend to Mantegna, and two years later her son, Cardinal Francesco Gonzaga, to whom the artist was devotedly attached, also passed away. When, in 1484, Federico himself died suddenly, and his eighteen-year-old son, Gian Francesco – generally referred to by his second name only – became Marquis in his stead, Mantegna seems to have feared that his position at Mantua would be adversely affected by all the changes that were taking place, and he hastened to offer his services to Lorenzo de' Medici, with whom he had some slight acquaintance, and whose liberality as a patron of art and literature was well known. What reply was made by the Florentine duke to his suggestion is not known; but it soon became evident that the new ruler of Mantua knew as well if not better than his father and grandfather had done before him, how to value his court painter, and one of the first acts of his reign was to ask Mantegna to paint a picture for him to present to the Duchess Eleonora of Mantua, mother of his affianced bride, Isabella d'Este, who was then only ten years old, but was later to become one of the artist's most liberal patrons and faithful admirers.

The picture in question is supposed to have been the fine "Madonna and Child," with a background of cherubs' heads, now in the Brera Gallery, Milan, considered, so far as its colouring is concerned, one of Mantegna's most brilliant achievements. According to some authorities, it had already been ordered some months before by the Duchess, and all Francesco had to do with it was to urge the artist to finish it without further delay; but, in any case, the young Marquis was constantly in the studio whilst it was in progress, chatting with the painter now about the work, now about his own private affairs. He was, it is said, deeply in love with his betrothed, or rather with the idea he had formed of her, for it is doubtful whether he had yet seen her, the wooing having been done by proxy as long previously as 1480, when the little maiden of six had delighted the Mantuan envoy with her grace and charm. No sooner was the picture signed, before the eager suitor had it packed, and started with it for Ferrara, where it was received with the greatest enthusiasm, not only by the Duchess herself but by the whole court, which, under the enlightened rule of Duke Ercole I. was a centre of culture, to which flocked artists, poets, musicians, humanists, and other leaders of the æsthetic and intellectual life of the day.

Of the actual meeting between the engaged couple no record has been preserved; but it is evident from letters written home by the Marquis that his expectations were more than fulfilled, Isabella already giving promise of the exceptional qualities which were to make her one of the most fascinating and influential women of her time, the memory of whose sweet and gracious presence still lingers both in Ferarra and Mantua. It was difficult for her lover to tear himself away when the day came for him to return home, where his presence was greatly needed; but before he left, he exacted a promise from Duchess Eleonora that she would bring her daughter to Mantua in the autumn of the same year.

It is easy to imagine how much Francesco had to confide to his court painter when he paid his next visit to the studio; how he dwelt on the charms of his beloved Isabella, and lamented over the years that must elapse before she could become his wife. He found Mantegna eagerly engaged on the preliminary drawings for the "Triumph of Cæsar," and to the instructions already given by Lodovico Gonzaga he added a wish that all the distinguished guests who were soon to meet at his court should be introduced in the processions, as well as the chief members of his own family. Mantegna, he may have said, would have plenty of opportunities for making studies of them; and now he must put everything else aside for a time to design the decorations in honour of the visit of the bride-elect and her mother, which were to be a kind of foretaste of those in celebration of the wedding. In all the preparations for that great event he relied upon the co-operation of Mantegna, who must promise not to accept any invitation or commission that could interfere with his work on them, and, premature as this must have appeared to the artist, he readily gave the required assurance.

All passed over as happily as Francesco himself could have wished during the brief stay at Mantua of Eleonora and Isabella, who won all hearts by their sympathetic appreciation of everything that was done to please them. After they left, the work on the "Triumph of Cæsar" proceeded apace, interrupted only now and then for the execution of minor commissions, such as the designing of jewellery, drinking-cups, &c.; but in 1488 came a very unwelcome summons for Mantegna to go to Rome, Pope Innocent VIII., who had heard of the beauty of the frescoes at Padua and Mantua, wishing to have a chapel in the Vatican decorated by their artist. Such an invitation had all the force of a command, and the Marquis was reluctantly compelled to let his beloved painter go; but before he left, he conferred on him the honour of knighthood, that he might take a better position in the papal court, and once more reminded him of the necessity that he should be back at Mantua in January 1490 at the very latest. Bearing with him a letter to the Pope, dated June 10, 1488, in which Francesco spoke of him in the very highest terms,

Mantegna started for the Holy City, where he was welcomed with the greatest eagerness, not only by his new employer but by the ecclesiastical and secular notabilities, who vied with each other in doing him honour. Certain letters to the Marquis Francesco, however, betray discontent with the payment he received from the Pope, and also with the facilities for his work afforded him in the Vatican, a dissatisfaction that would, indeed, have been intensified could he have foreseen that the frescoes for which he sacrificed so much were to be ruthlessly destroyed in 1780, with the chapel containing them, to make room for the Museo Pio Clementina.

It is only from allusions to them by Vasari and descriptions by the later critics, Agostino Taja and Giovanni Pietro Chattard, who lived in the second half of the eighteenth century, and saw the frescoes shortly before their destruction, that any idea can be obtained of what they were; but a supposed copy of a portrait of Innocent VIII. included in them, is in the collection of the Archduke Ferdinand of Austria. That they were executed by Mantegna without any assistance is proved by a letter from him to the Marquis Francesco, dated June 15, 1489, in which he says, "The work is heavy for a man alone, intent on obtaining honours, especially in Rome, where opinion is expressed by so many able men, and as in the races run by Barbary horses the first gets the prize, so I too must gain in the end, if it please God."

It is unnecessary to dwell long on works of art that have completely disappeared. Suffice it to say that the frescoes were not finished in December 1489, but that Mantegna was hoping to get leave of absence from the Pope for February 1490, when he was suddenly struck down by fever, just before he would have started for Mantua had all been well. The long-talked-of wedding took place, therefore, during his absence, and he had, after all, absolutely nothing to do with the festivities in honour of the marriage, that were evidently of a magnificent description. It must have been, indeed, a keen mortification to him to have missed such a golden opportunity of proving his devotion to his

Mantuan patron, and it is easy to realise with what mixed feelings he heard of the enthusiastic reception of the bride in her husband's native city. Accompanied by Isabella's parents, her uncle Cardinal d'Este, and her three young brothers, and escorted by a brilliant suite, the newly wedded pair entered the city on February 12th, the one drawback to their happiness, contemporary chroniclers report, having been the absence of the court painter, whose praises had been so often sung by the bridegroom.

Fortunately, the artist soon recovered from his illness, but it was not until September that he completed his work in Rome, and received permission from the Pope to return to Mantua. Innocent VIII. expressed himself in his letter of dismissal fully satisfied with the way in which his wishes had been carried out; but whether the artist was equally pleased with the reward for his services is questionable. He was evidently very glad to leave Rome, where, strange to say, in spite of his love for antiquity and the opportunities he must have enjoyed for his favourite study, he seems to have felt out of his element. His correspondence with the Marquis betrays considerable home-sickness, and contains absolutely no allusions to the art treasures of the Vatican. He pleads with his patron for an appointment for his son Lodovico, declares he is longing to be at work again on the "Triumph of Cæsar," and retails various items of court gossip, telling quaint stories, for instance, about the ill-fated Prince Djem, brother of the reigning Sultan of Turkey, who was then a prisoner in the Vatican, but not a word does he say to throw light on the political situation, which was already causing anxiety to the heads of the great Italian states. Back again in Mantua, Mantegna quickly threw off the depression revealed in his letters, resuming his old place as if he had never been away, his studio becoming once more the centre of artistic activity in the ancient town.

The court painter was as eagerly welcomed by the young Marchesa as by her husband, and for the rest of his life his fortunes were very closely bound up with those of the d'Este family, which is equivalent to saying that he was henceforth to be in close touch with the history of his native country, that was even then on the eve of the Revolution that was completely to change her position in the polity of nations. The Marquis of Mantua's bride was the only sister of Beatrice d'Este, who was married on December 29, 1490, to the brilliantly gifted but fickle, cruel, and crafty Lodovico Sforza, surnamed Il Moro, who obtained the dukedom of Milan through treachery, and was mainly instrumental in bringing about the invasion of Italy by the French, a crime for which he was to pay dearly, first with his liberty and in the end with his life, for he died a prisoner in the Castle of Loches in 1508.

No hint of troubles to come saddened the first few months of Isabella d'Este's life at Mantua, her chief anxiety having apparently been concerning her beloved sister, whose lot was far less happy than her own. Lodovico Sforza had not been nearly so ardent a lover as Francesco Gonzaga, for he had a mistress, the lovely and learned Cecilia Gallerani, to whom he was devotedly attached, and who had been for many years treated by him as if she were his legal wife. It is significant of the indulgent manner in which such unions were regarded that his relations with her were not considered any bar to his marriage with an innocent young girl, whose parents did all in their power to hasten her engagement with him. It was very evident, however, that Beatrice did not share their eagerness, and it was to Isabella, who had hastened to Ferrara as soon as the matter was settled, that she turned for comfort in her shrinking dread of what was before her. That the Marchesa succeeded in reassuring her and bracing her up for the ordeal is proved by the dignified way in which the child-bride bore herself in the long-drawn-out and brilliant festivities that celebrated her union with a man more than double her own age, and the ease with which she took up the arduous duties of the wife of the leading and most powerful prince of Italy. It was with a heart relieved of its most pressing fears that the elder sister returned home, and the letters written to her by

Beatrice in the months succeeding her departure reveal a growing attachment between the newly married couple, on which a seal was set in January 1493 by the birth of their first son.

The court of the Gonzagas now became the rendezvous of the leading authors, artists, and antiquarians of the day, who vied with each other in their enthusiastic admiration for the beautiful young Marchesa, though it is occasionally suggested by contemporary writers that as time went on some of them rather rebelled against her increasing exactions, for she would fain have had every one give up everything to obey her behests. She is even said to have sent imperious messages to such great celebrities as Perugino, Giovanni Bellini, and Leonardo da Vinci, bidding them come and help Mantegna to decorate her apartments, describing the subjects she wished them to interpret, and expressing herself as greatly aggrieved when they failed to appear. On the other hand, there is no doubt that she proved herself a most generous and considerate patron of her own court painter, and the four years after his return from Rome were probably among the happiest of Mantegna's life.

He worked during them almost exclusively at the "Triumph of Cæsar," receiving no help from any other artist, completing the tenth composition in 1494, and making several sketches for others that were never finished. In these wonderful creations the artist realised the very spirit of antiquity, yet at the same time bequeathed to posterity a marvellously true series of presentments of the contemporary life of his time, full of significant incidents and effective contrasts, the various groups displaying a freedom of execution and force of expression such as Mantegna had never before achieved. For the first time realism and idealism were welded into one, and the past seemed actually to become the present, waking into new life not merely as an intellectual abstraction, but as a visible pageant of humanity.

The year of the successful conclusion of the "Triumph of Cæsar" was a disastrous one for Italy, for in July 1494 the Duke of Orleans, on the invitation of Lodovico Sforza, crossed the Alps, to be followed almost immediately by Charles VIII. The French King and the Duke of Orleans were welcomed with great enthusiasm by Il Moro, whose wife wrote glowing accounts to her sister at Mantua of the rejoicings over their arrival; but those who looked below the surface recognised what a fatal mistake had been made, and sinister rumours soon began to spread abroad as to the real motives of Lodovico Sforza. The death of his nephew Giangaleazzo at a most opportune moment for him led to suspicions of his having caused him to be poisoned, that were confirmed by the way in which he managed to get his claim to the succession recognised and the dead man's young son Francesco set aside in his own favour. For all that, he was allowed to assume the supreme authority at Milan without opposition, and contemporary chroniclers even comment on the kindness shown by him and his wife to the widowed duchess, to whom apartments were assigned in the palace that had so long been her home. Meanwhile, everything had remained quiet at Mantua, though all that was going on elsewhere was being watched with eager interest by the Gonzagas and Mantegna. Early in 1495 Isabella went to Milan to be with her sister, who was expecting her second child, and on February 4th a fine boy was born. In the brilliant festivities held to celebrate the great event the child's beautiful aunt is said to have taken a leading part, now receiving ambassadors from foreign courts to save the young mother fatigue, now advising her brother-in-law in some difficult question of etiquette, capping verses with Gaspare Visconti, criticising the work of Giovanni Bellini, or playing with her two-year-old nephew, Ercole, who simply worshipped her.

Suddenly, in the midst of all this light-hearted gaiety, came the news that Charles VIII. had entered Naples and been crowned King of Sicily, and though the bells of Milan were ostentatiously rung as if in rejoicing, a council was hastily summoned to consult on the best measures to save Italy from the French invaders. On April 12th a league against France was signed between Venice, Urbino, Mantua, Milan, King Ferdinand of Spain and the

Emperor Maximilian; the Marquis of Mantua was made Generalissimo of the united Italian forces, and after taking an affectionate farewell of Mantegna, who, he said, would soon be called upon to paint a masterpiece in celebration of a victory, he set forth in high spirits at the head of his army. His words turned out to be prophetic, for on July 6th, at Fornovo, he defeated the French with great loss, fighting himself side by side with his soldiers in the front rank. Before he went into action he vowed that if he escaped unhurt he would build a church in honour of the Virgin at Mantua, and as soon as the battle was over he sent instructions to Mantegna to make plans of the building, and to design an altar-piece for it.

The church was finished before the painting, which was not begun until August 30th, but it was completed in time to be placed in position on the anniversary of the event it commemorated, and is universally considered the artist's finest work of the kind, surpassing even the beautiful S. Zeno triptych. It is now one of the chief treasures of the Louvre, having been taken to France in 1797, and is known as the "Madonna della Vittoria," although, as a matter of fact, it represents the Marquis of Mantua pleading with the Virgin for the success of his arms, not returning thanks for victory, the whole composition breathing forth yearning aspiration rather than exultation. In it the Holy Child occupies the centre of the design, all the light being concentrated on Him and on the face of His mother, who embraces Him with one hand, and stretches forth the other towards the kneeling suppliant, opposite to whom are St. Elizabeth and the Infant St. John the Baptist. The mantle of the Virgin is held back by Saints George and Michael, and against the ornate background appear the heads of the patrons of Mantua, Saints Andrew and Longinus, the whole being admirably proportioned and well balanced.

During the years that succeeded the victory of Fornovo the Marquis of Mantua and his wife had to contend not only with great political anxieties but with one of the greatest sorrows of their lives – the sudden death of the Duchess of Milan, who passed away on January 2, 1497, after giving birth to a still-born son. Her end is said to have been hastened by the fact that her husband, who had hitherto seemed devoted to her, had recently conceived a passion for a lovely girl named Lucrezia Crivelli, who had been one of her ladies-in-waiting. However that may have been, Lodovico's grief at her loss, intensified perhaps by self-reproach, was extreme, and the letter he wrote to his brother-in-law asking him to break the terrible news to Isabella is one long cry of anguish. That the young wife had been mercifully taken away from the evil to come soon, however, became apparent, for before she had been dead a year her husband's doom was already sealed. Heavy clouds, too, were gathering at Mantua, for the Marquis fell under the suspicion of having had underhand dealings with the enemy, and in April 1497 he was suddenly dismissed from his post as Generalissimo of the Italian forces. This was a bitter blow to him, to his wife, and to all, including Mantegna, who had his interests at heart, but fortunately the storm quickly blew over, and he was soon restored to his command, which he retained to the end of the campaign.

The taking of Milan by the French in 1499 and the triumphant entry into the conquered city of Louis XII. – who, the little dauphin having died shortly before his father, had become King of France on the death of Charles VIII. – with all the terrible consequences to the Sforza family, cast a gloom over the court of Mantua for the rest of the reign of the Marquis Francesco, and both he and Isabella found their best distraction from their many sorrows in watching their court painter at work. The "Madonna della Vittoria" was succeeded by the "Madonna with Saints and Angels," now in the collection of Prince Trivulzio at Milan, painted for the monks of S. Maria in Organo, Verona, and the "Madonna and Child with St. John the Baptist," now in the National Gallery, with the smaller but no less charming "Holy Family" of the Dresden Gallery. To about the same period are supposed to belong the designs for the frescoes in Mantegna's mortuary chapel in S. Andrea, Mantua, of which only two – the "Holy Family with St. Elizabeth, Zacharias, and the Infant St. John" and the "Baptism of Christ," the latter almost defaced – are from the hand of the master himself, the rest having been completed after his death by his pupils.

In 1500, when Andrea was already in his seventieth year, he was commissioned by the Marchesa to paint a series of allegorical subjects in what she called her "studio," in the Castello of Mantua, on the decoration of which several other artists, including Perugino and Lorenzo da Costa, were also engaged. Mantegna was, unfortunately, the only one of the painters selected who approached the task with any enthusiasm, or attempted to realise the ambition of Isabella – that her sanctum should be a kind of epitome of intellectual and sensuous life, symbolising, as do the Trifoni of Petrarch in literature, the most ideal aspirations of humanity. The first of the compositions completed by Mantegna was the "Parnassus," in which the conquest of Mars by Venus is celebrated, that is unique amongst the master's works, generally characterised as they are by sobriety of expression, as an interpretation of light-hearted gaiety. The figures of the dancing-girls are full of vivacious grace, and that of the Goddess of Love of seductive charm, contrasting well with the virile and heroic form of her suitor, the stern God of War, whilst the minor actors in the idyllic scene – the neglected husband, Vulcan, working at his forge as if indifferent to what is going on, Apollo, Mercury, and Cupid – are all most happily rendered, the various groups combining to give the impression of a living drama, in which the artist, in the fulness of his creative power, for once succeeded in giving visible expression to his lifelong dream of the old Olympus, which he had previously seen only in his imagination.

It was not until some years after the execution of the "Parnassus" that the second of the "studio" pictures, the comparatively uninteresting "Triumph of Virtue over the Vices," was finished. Though its details were evidently carefully studied, it shows a lamentable falling off in simplicity and effectiveness of design, Mantegna having been greatly hampered by the constant interference of Isabella, who insisted on the introduction of a bewildering number of allegorical figures. The third and last composition, an equally unpromising subject, the "Triumph of Erotic Love," was only begun by Andrea, and completed by Lorenzo da Costa, who faithfully endeavoured to fulfil his predecessor's intentions. All three paintings are now in the Louvre, where the "Parnassus" may be usefully compared with the earlier "Madonna della Vittoria" and the "Crucifixion," the three works being very typical of the various periods of the master's development.

To 1506 belongs the fine and characteristic monochrome decorative picture of the "Triumph of Scipio," now in the National Gallery, one of the very latest of the master's works, commemorating two important episodes of the second Punic War – the welcome given to the image of the goddess Cybele brought from Rome to Ostia by Publius Scipio, and the miracle wrought by the "Mother of the Gods" on her arrival, which proved the innocence of the Roman matron, Claudia Quinta, who had been falsely accused of immorality. Concerning this fine work, in which the artist tells the well-known classic story with dramatic directness, a very interesting correspondence has been preserved, between Isabella d'Este and the famous Venetian scholar, Pietro Bembo, who complained to the Marchioness that Mantegna had long ago pledged himself to paint certain pictures for his friend, Francesco Cornaro, who had paid twenty-five ducats on account. He begged the master's patroness to induce him to fulfil his engagements, adding that "Messer Cornaro would not mind about a couple of hundred ducats; he would gladly leave the value of the pictures to her, but he would not allow himself to be jested with, and meant to stand upon his rights." To this the great lady appealed to replied that "she would certainly speak for Cornaro to Mantegna when opportunity should occur, but that the aged artist was at the moment scarcely recovered from a serious illness, so that it was impossible yet to talk to him about business." That she did intervene soon afterwards, or that Mantegna's own conscience reproached him, is, however, proved by the fact that the completed "Triumph of Scipio" was found in his studio after his death.

The picture is referred to by the painter's son Lodovico in a letter to the Marchioness "as that work of Scipio Cornelio which was undertaken for Messer Francesco Cornaro, and which the Cardinal Sigismondo Gonzaga desired to retain for himself." Vainly did Andrea's second son protest against this, begging the Marquis Francesco to let him have it back, "for he wished to keep it as a memorial of his father and for purposes of study," a plea delightfully suggestive of happy relations having existed between the writer and the great master. Francesco Mantegna added that he would gladly pay back the twenty-five ducats to Cornaro, and great was his disappointment when, after a long delay, he received as sole answer to his request a promissory note from the Cardinal for one hundred ducats, which in the end turned out to be no more than waste paper, for as long afterwards as November 1507 neither he nor his brother had been able to get the money. In the end, the descendants of Messer Cornaro got possession of the picture, which was bought from one of them by Lord George Vivian, whose son left it to the National Gallery in 1873.

With the "Triumph of Scipio" may justly be ranked the "Samson and Delilah," also now in the National Gallery, that is evidently entirely from the hand of the master himself, and is a very realistic interpretation of the much-exploited incident of the betrayal of the strong man by the weak but cunning woman. Other typical drawings are the "Judgment of Solomon," in the Louvre, and the three renderings of Judith placing the head of Holofernes in a sack that is held open by her handmaiden – one in the possession of Mr. John Taylor, one at Dublin, and the third in the Uffizi. The last, signed by the artist with his full name and dated 1491, is a truly admirable rendering of its subject, the shrinking horror felt by the beautiful and heroic girl of the ghastly trophy she is about to let fall, being vividly reflected in her attitude and expression as well as in those of her companion. Less satisfactory from a technical point of view are the "Mutius Scævola" of the Munich collection, commemorative of the noble deed of the young Roman who had been chosen by lot to slay the Etruscan invader, King Porsenna, and having failed was condemned to be burnt alive; the group of "Mars, Venus, and Diana," in the British Museum; the "Vestal Virgin Tucia," also known as "Autumn," and the "Greek Woman drinking from a Cup," sometimes called "Summer," in the National Gallery. Even they, however, as well as the more important drawings, are eminently characteristic of their author, who from first to last was more pictorial in his sketches than in his finished compositions.

Not only as a painter but as an engraver did Mantegna win great renown during his lifetime and abiding fame after his death. He and his gifted contemporary, Antonio Pollaiuolo, were the first Italians to employ copperplate engravings for original work and the reproduction of their drawings, and a very great impulse was given by them to the useful craft.

The closing months of Mantegna's life are involved in an obscurity as great as that shrouding his early years. It is not even known of what he died, some saying that he was suddenly carried off by the plague which was raging in Mantua at the time, others that the end had long been expected, and that old age was his only ailment. The sad event took place at seven o'clock in the evening, on September 13, 1506, and the news was formally notified to the Marquis two days later by Francesco Mantegna; but, probably because of the great anxieties by which the Gonzagas were then oppressed, very little notice was taken of what under other circum stances would have overwhelmed them with grief.

Andrea Mantegna was quietly buried in the chapel in S. Andrea, Mantua, that he had long since secured as the last resting-place of his family, and which, except for the completion of the unfinished frescoes, remains to the present day very much what it was at the time of his death. It was not until fifty years later that the bronze bust, already referred to, was set up outside the chapel by his grandson Andrea, son of Lodovico Mantegna, who also erected within the building a fine memorial to his grandfather, father, and uncle, bearing the inscription, "Ossa Andreæ Mantineæ famosissimi pictoris cum duobus filiis in hoc sepulcro per Andream Mantineæ nepotem ex filio constructo reposita MDLX."

In addition to the well-authenticated paintings, frescoes, and engravings described above, a very great number of other works, including easel pictures, drawings, and miniatures, have been attributed to Mantegna, who is also said to have occasionally practised sculpture. Moreover, literary evidence proves that nearly one hundred compositions designed and executed by him have been lost, amongst which are specially to be regretted the portraits of his various patrons of the Gonzaga family and, above all, that of the Duchess Elizabetta of Urbino, who was one of the most beautiful and influential women of her time, beloved by young and old, and for whom her brilliant sister-in-law, Isabella d'Este, had a most fervent admiration. Even without these missing treasures, however, the court painter of Mantua left behind him masterpieces enough to secure to him a lasting fame as one of the pioneers of the Renaissance of painting in Italy.

The fact that Mantegna passed away on the very threshold of the Golden Age, during which Leonardo da Vinci, Michael Angelo, Raphael, Titian, and Correggio, each the founder of a great school, produced their world-famous works, has led to his achievements having been comparatively neglected; but of late years his claims have gradually become more fully recognised, and he now takes high rank as a consistent and persevering exponent of a high ideal. His intense individuality was from the first hostile to imitation, but his influence was long felt in the art world, and many artists who were associated with him in Padua and Mantua later carried on his traditions to some extent in Verona, Ferrara, Modena, Bologna, and Milan. Jacopo da Montagnana was, perhaps, the master who most closely resembled him, some of his work having been actually attributed to Mantegna; but Francesco Benaglio, Liberate da Verona, Francesco Moroni, Girolamo dai Libri, Marco Zoppo, Cosimo Tura, and Lorenzo da Costa owed much to their study of his masterpieces – the last named, who succeeded him as court painter at Mantua, reproducing in his later compositions something of the characteristic style of his predecessor in that office.

It has even been claimed that Correggio, who, according to a long-accepted but now dis credited tradition, was supposed to have been the actual pupil of Mantegna, derived much of his inspiration from the older painter. "Both artists," says Dr. Kristeller in an able examination of the points of affinity between them, "penetrate to the very core of the subject, to the purely human emotion latent within it: equally sensitive and elevated in spirit, both strive enthusiastically after a superhuman existence, full of an enhanced joy in life.... Both seek to break through the confines of the earthly to secure, in immeasurable space, free scope for the power and the magnitude of their figures. The voluptuous swinging lines, the ideally beautiful forms of Mantegna's figures in his later works, their sweet and thoughtful expression of tranquil bliss and spiritual emotion is in Correggio's creations only heightened by the passionate sensuousness of his own outlook on the world, by the utmost vivacity of movement, and by his ardent surrender of self to the sensuous as well as to the godlike. But," adds the German critic, and here he lays his finger on the essential difference between the art and character of the men compared, "sensuousness in Mantegna was neither ignored nor emphasised," for there was no pandering to the love of sensation in the work of the sincere and earnest master of Mantua, who never represented passion for its own sake, but combined with a true appreciation of the beauty of physical form and the poetry of motion a stern severity of expression peculiarly his own. Both masters pursued the same ideal of beauty, both penetrated to the very heart of their subjects, but the paintings of

Mantegna are more elevated in spirit than those of the more widely admired successor, whose forerunner he is said to have been.

There is, it must be admitted, a certain want of dramatic unity marring the effect even of the greatest compositions of the Mantuan painter; but it should not be forgotten that his aim was not the same as that of Raphael, Titian, Holbein, or Memlinc. Even his severest critics are compelled to admit that he fully realised his own ambition, a truly worthy one, to bring the past into touch with the present, and to pave the way for those who should come after him. His best works display not only consummate draughtsmanship but a power of interpreting intellectual and spiritual emotion, rare amongst his contemporaries, though it was to be bestowed in fullest measure upon many of the masters of the sixteenth century; and he will ever remain, in the opinion of those most competent to judge, one of the greatest of their predecessors.

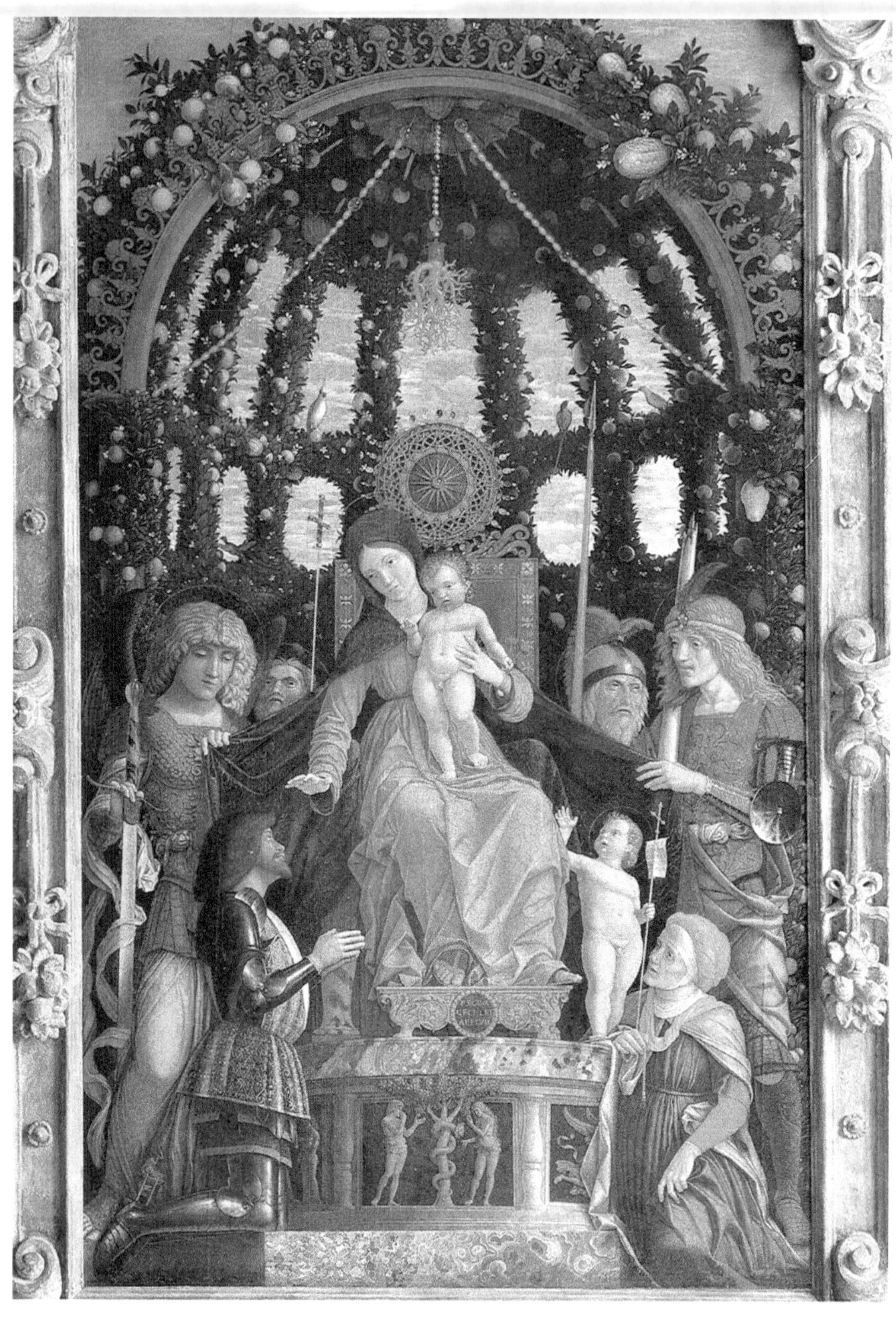

Andrea Mantegna, Madonna della Vittoria
(this page and over)

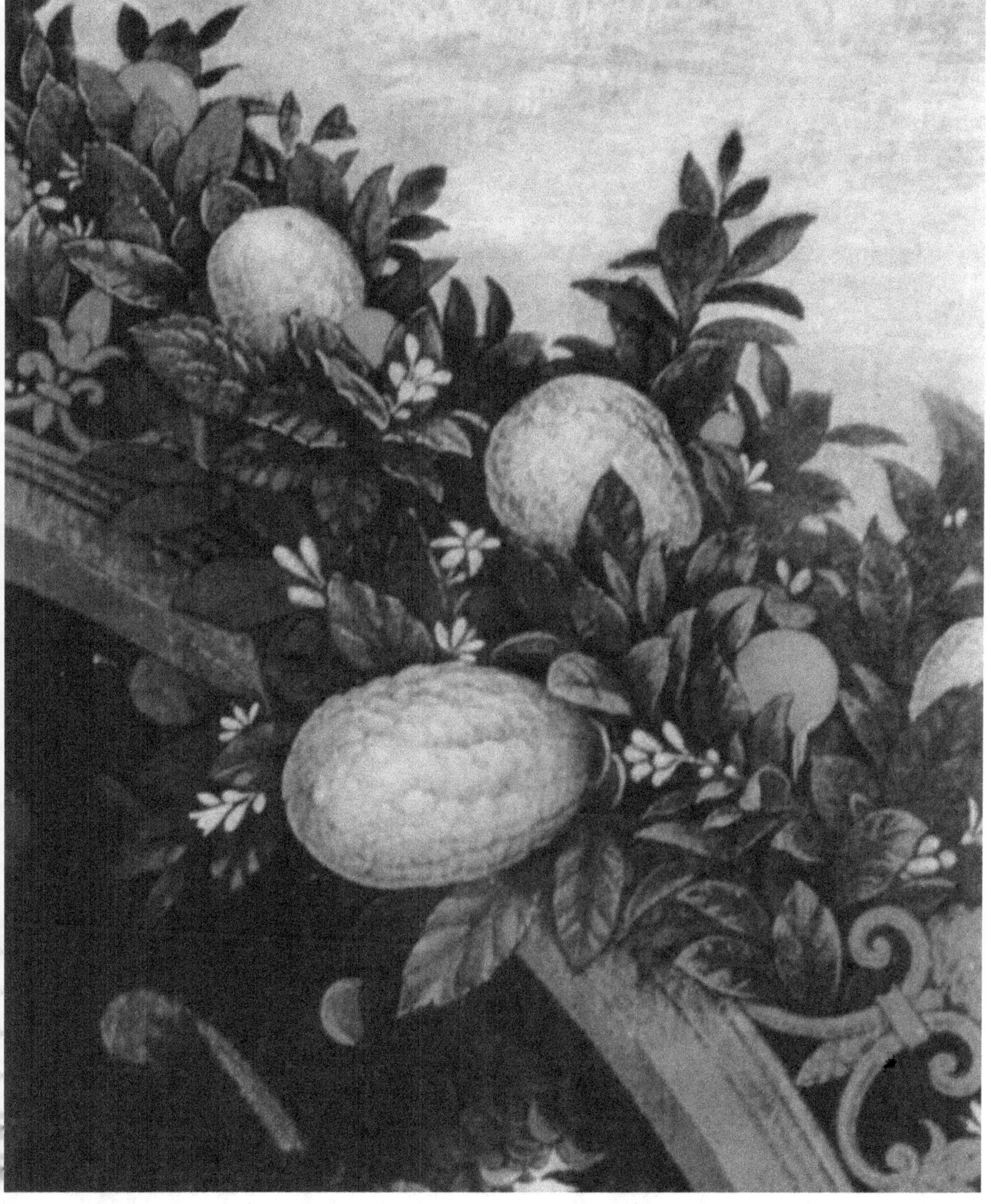

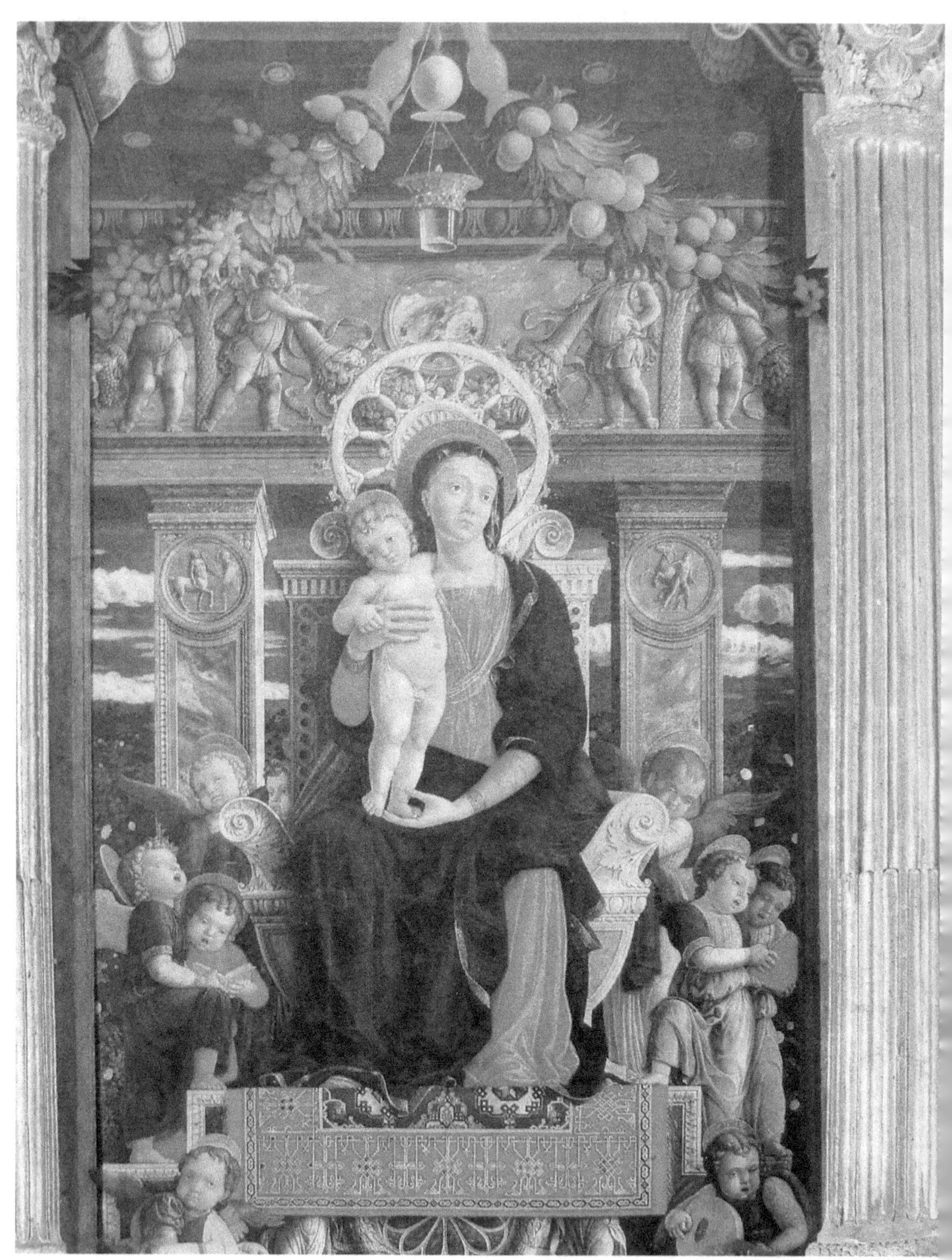

Andreas Mantegna, Madonna and Child Enthroned, 1457-60, Verona

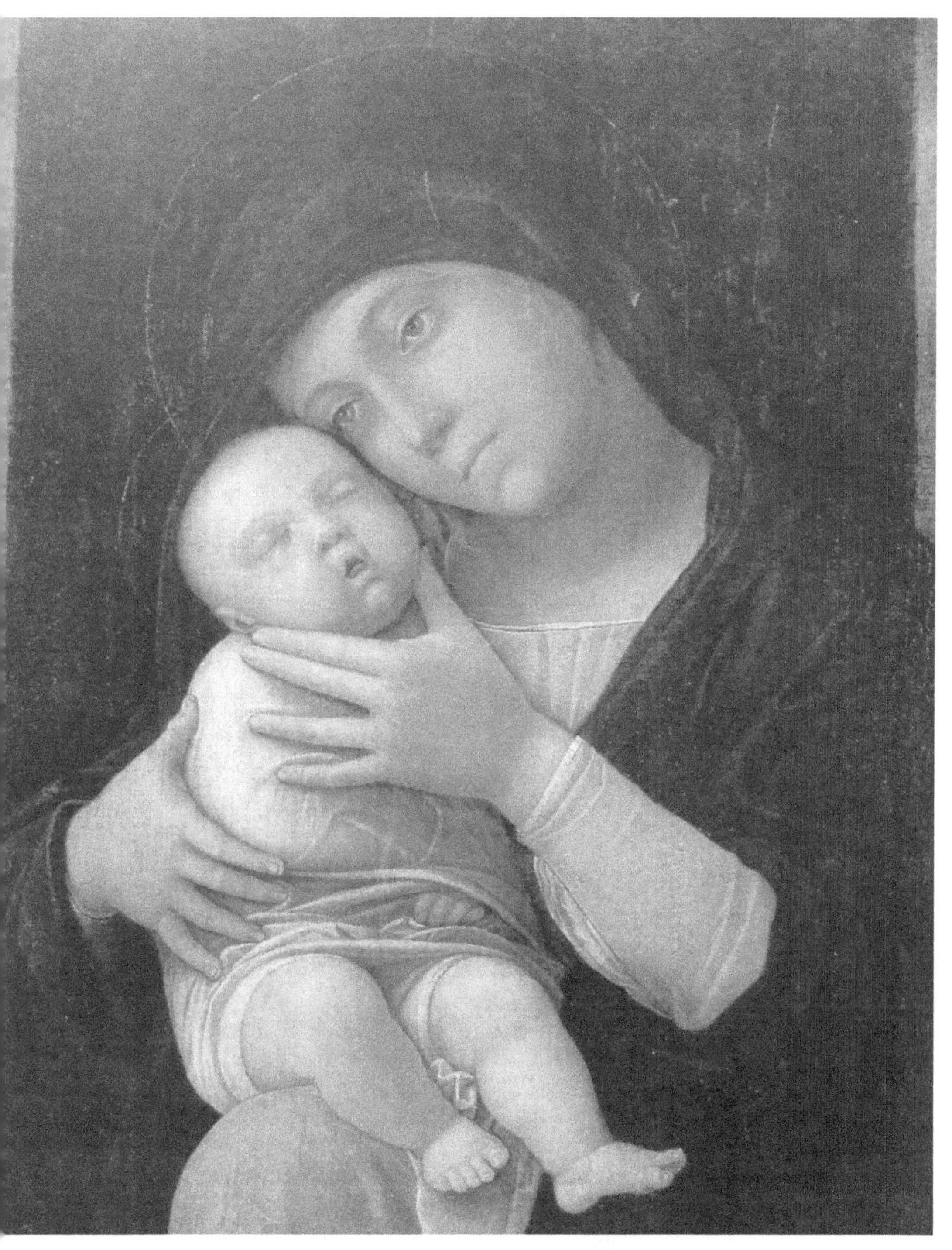

Andrea Mantegna, Virgin and Child, Milan

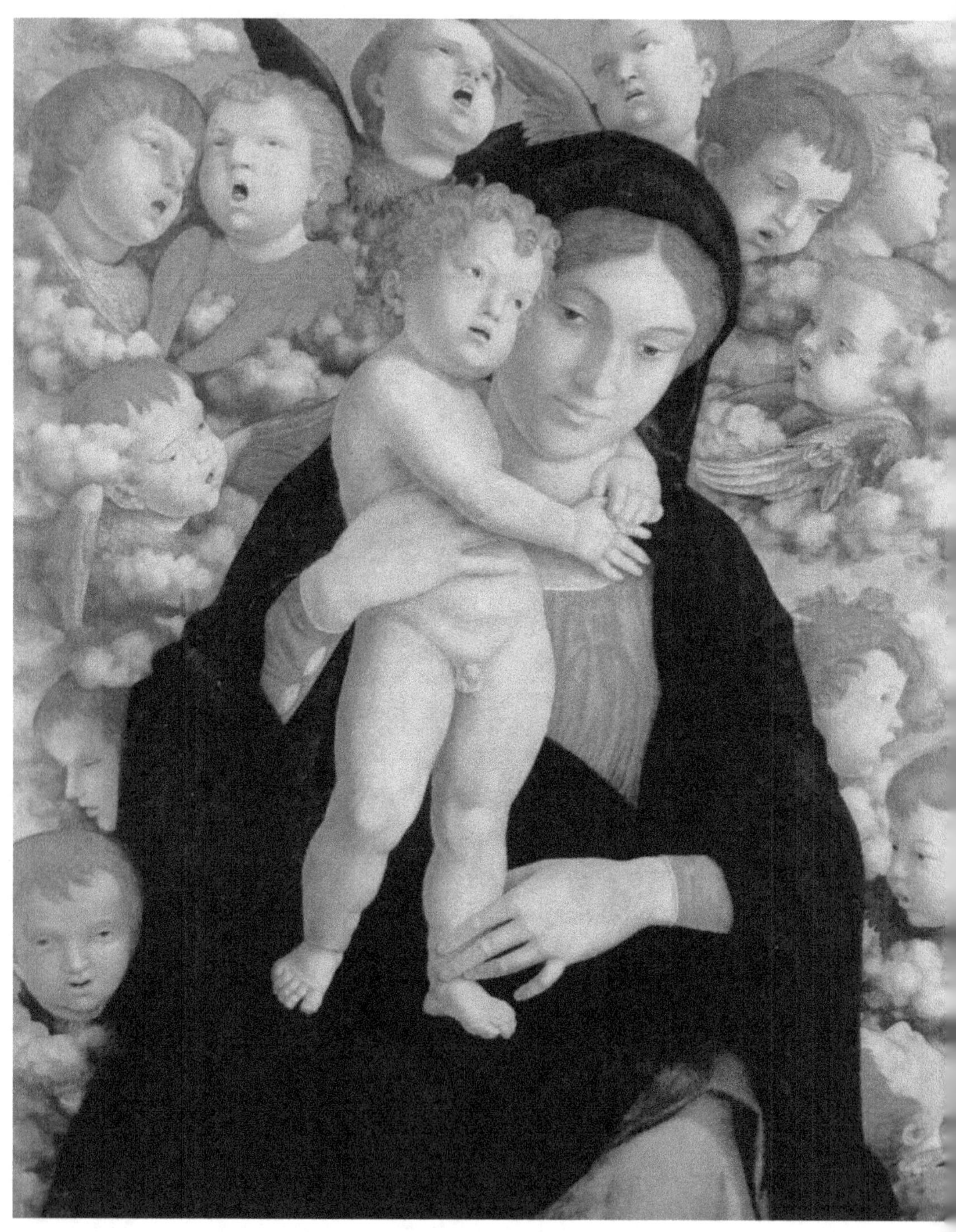

Andrea Mantegna, Madonna and Child, 1485, Milan

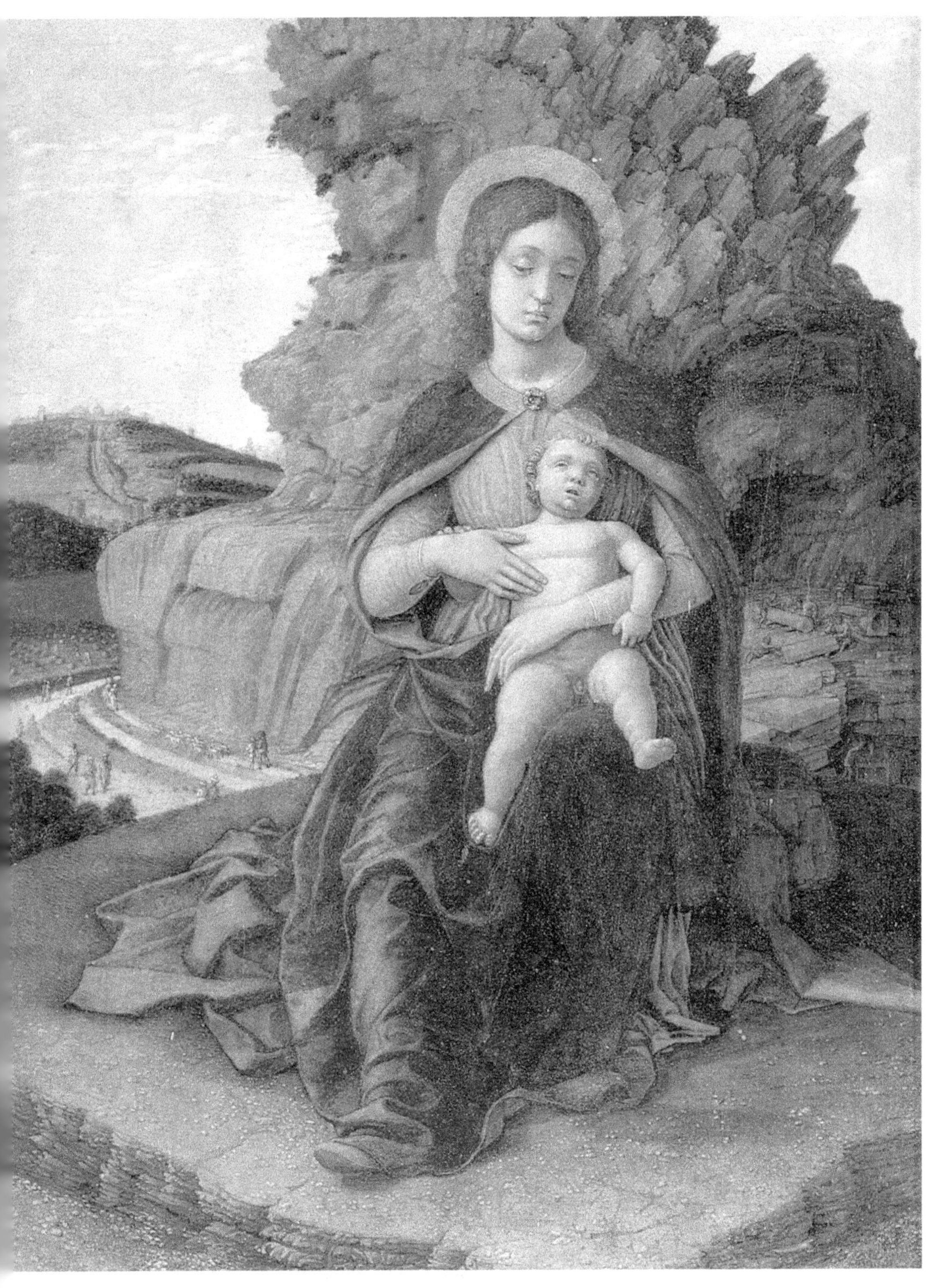

Andrea Mantegna, Madonna of the Grotto, Uffizi Gallery,

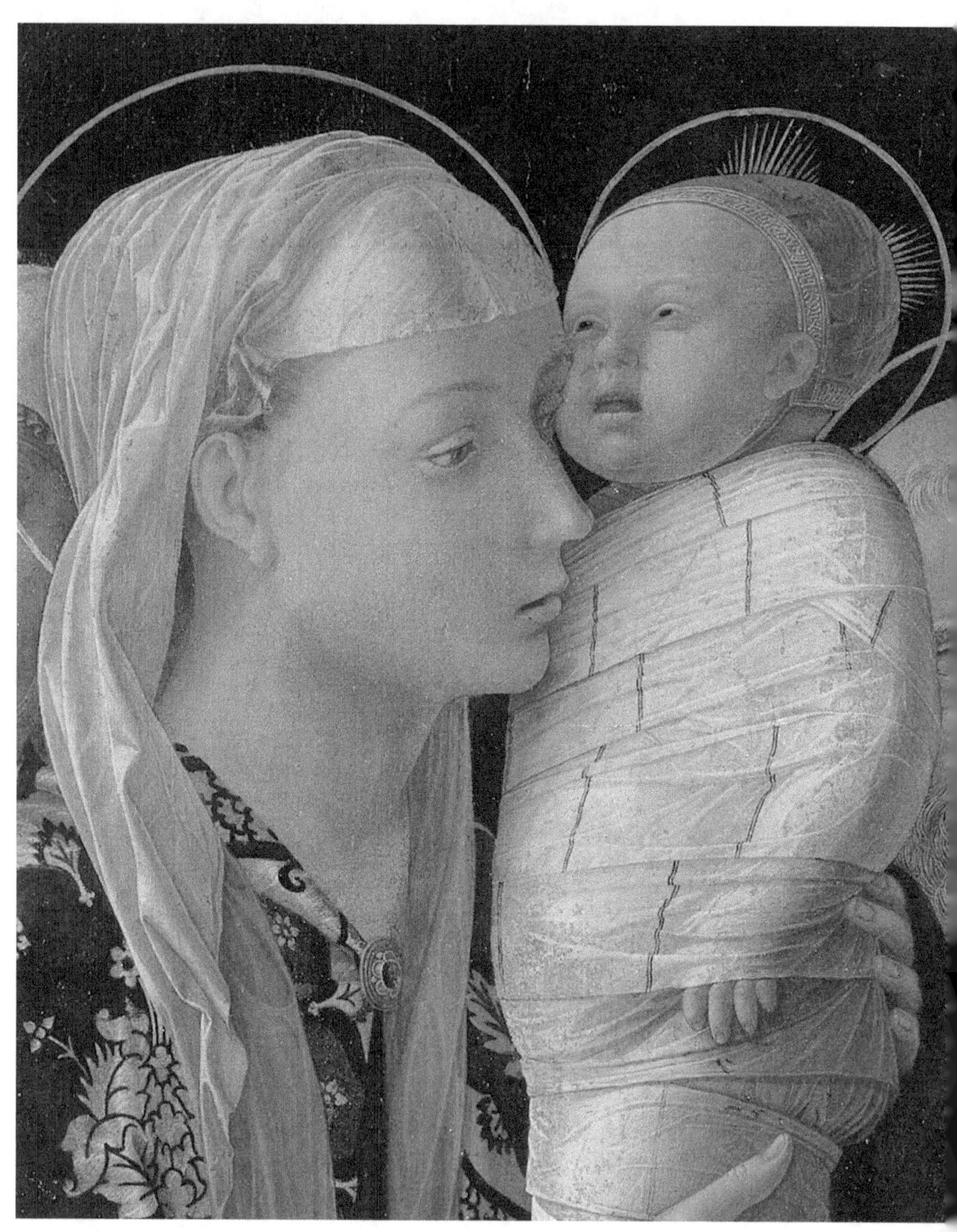

Andrea Mantegna, Tondo, Uffizi Gallery

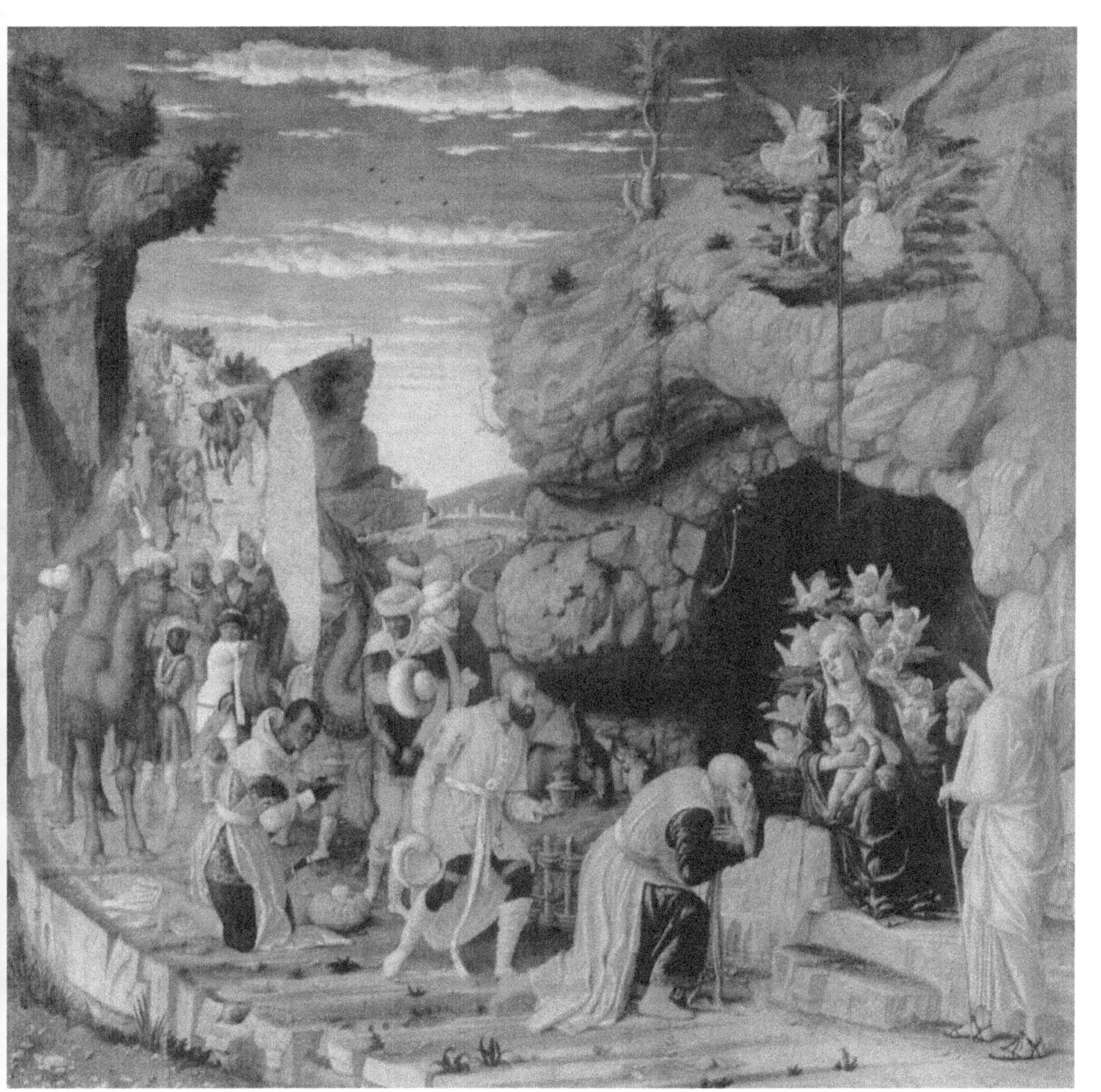

Andrea Mantegna, Adoration of the Magi, Uffizi Gallery

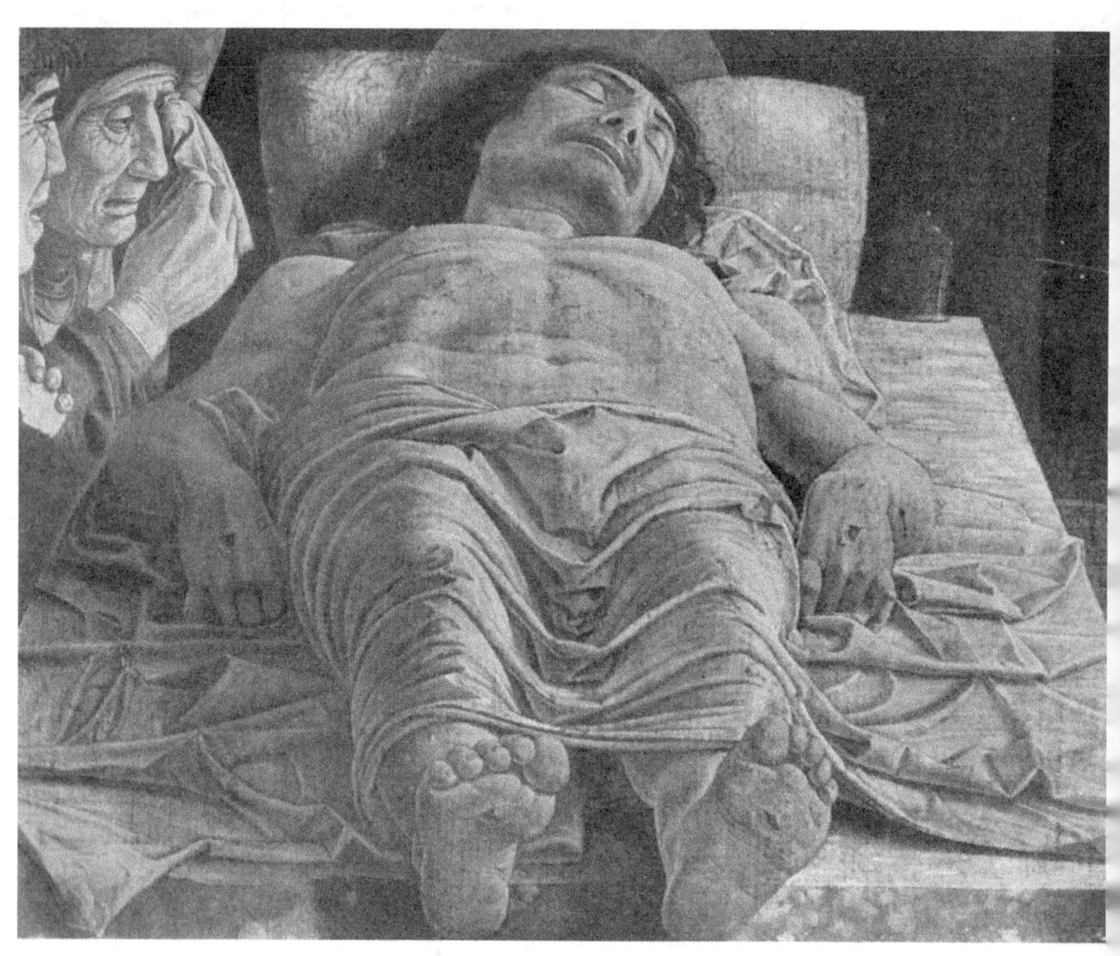

Andrea Mantegna, Lamentation Over the Dead Christ, 1470-74, Milan

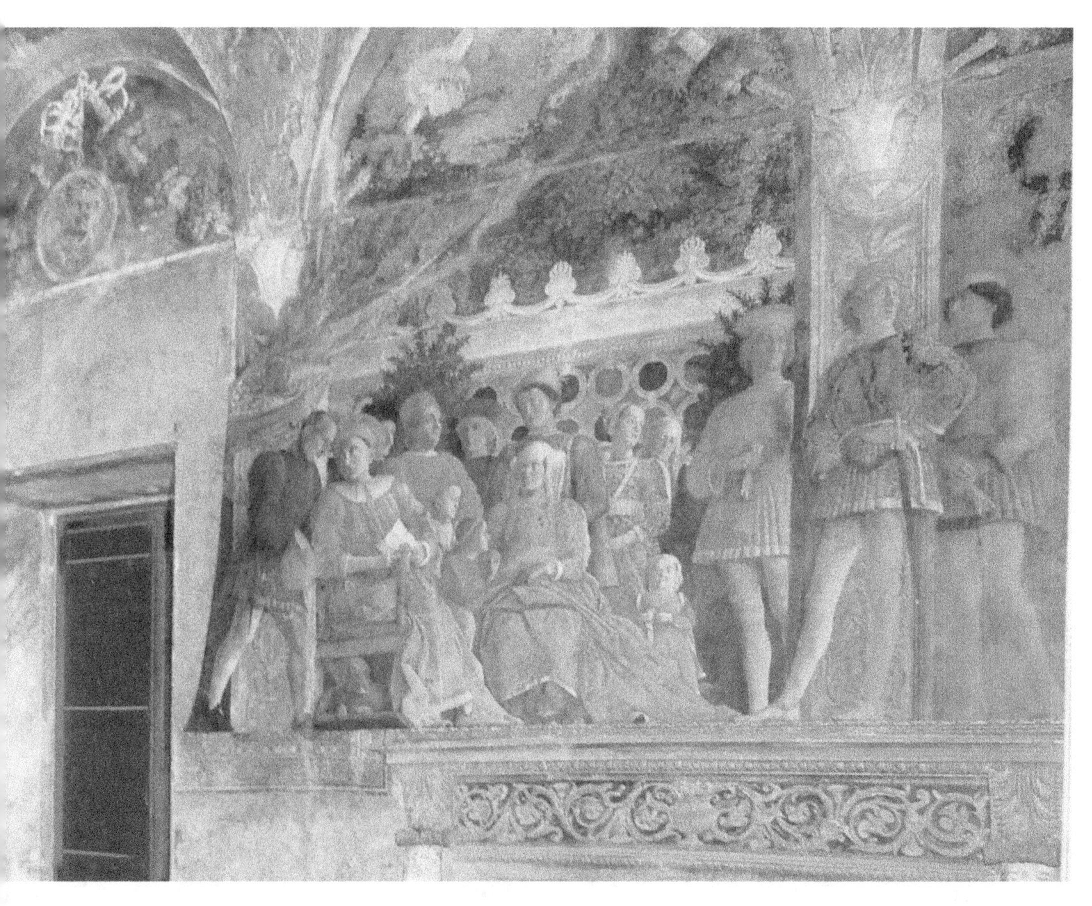

Andrea Mantegna, Palazzo Ducale, Mantua

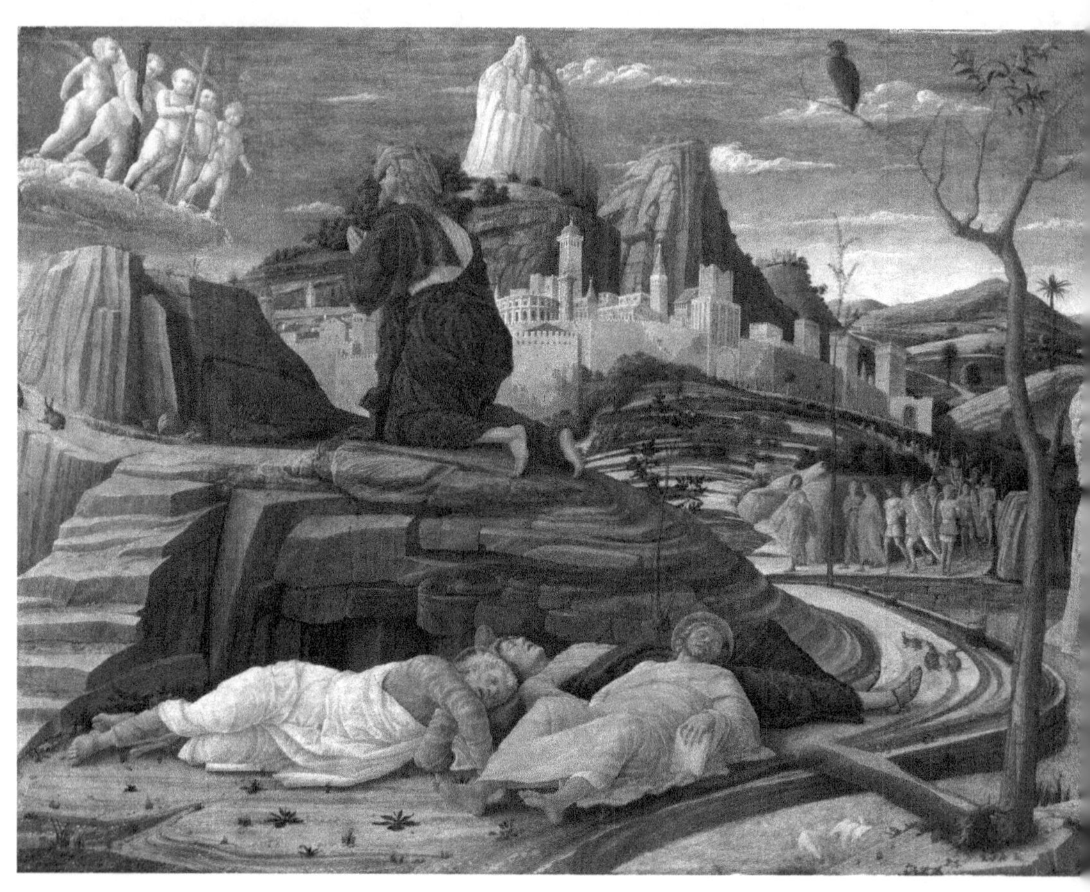

Andrea Mantegna, Agony In the Garden, 1458-60,
National Gallery, London

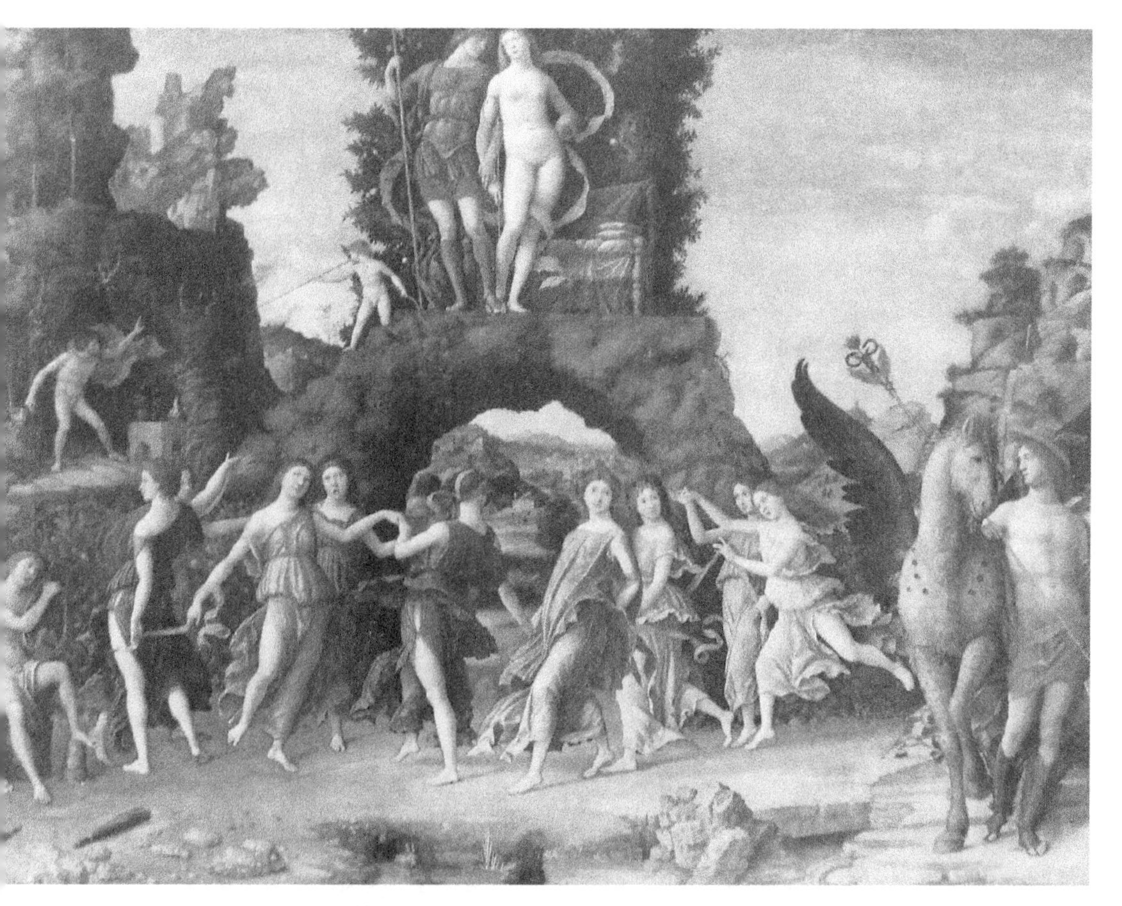

Andrea Mantegna, Mars and Venus, 1497

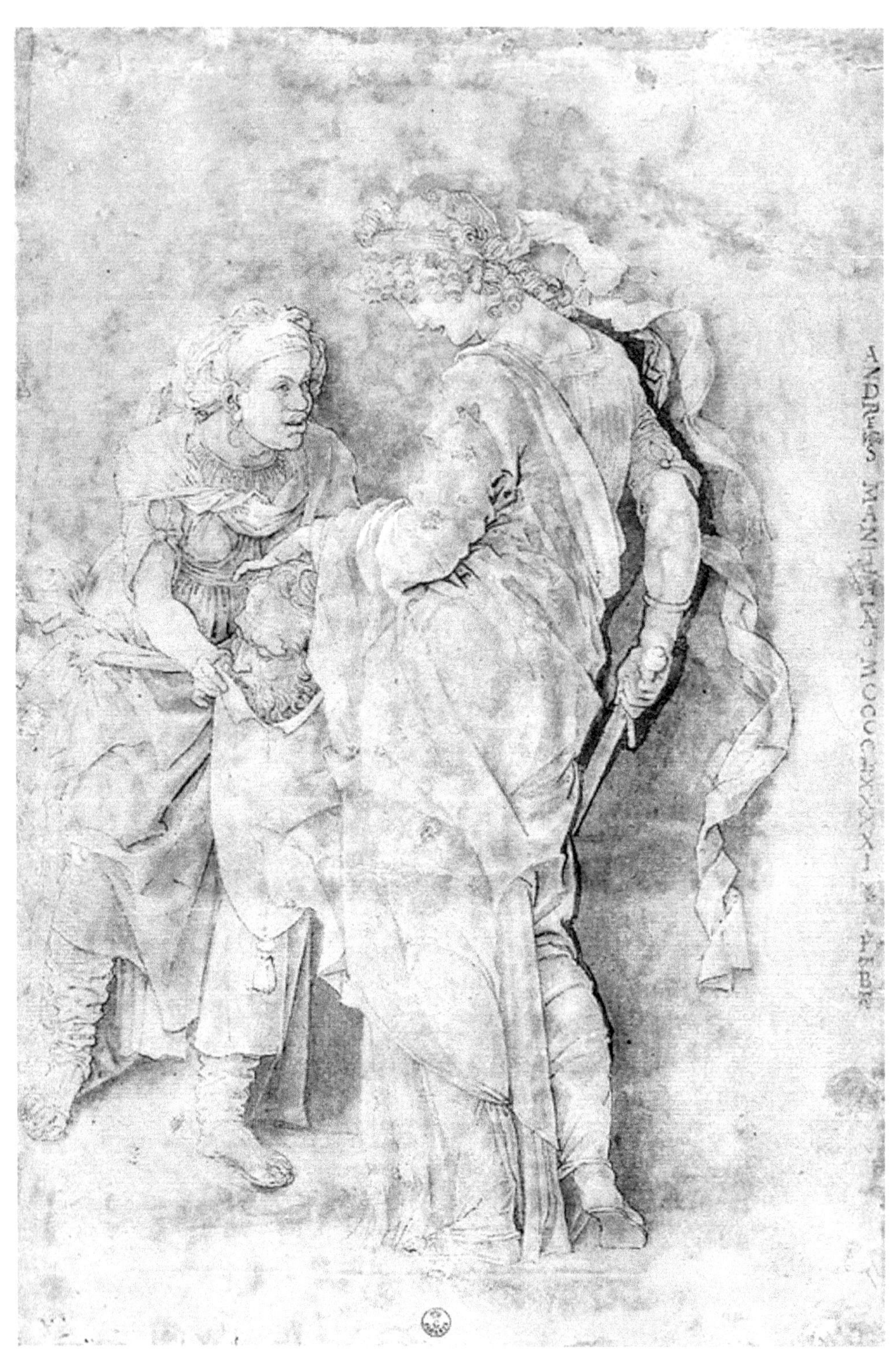

Andrea Mantegna, Study, Uffizi Gallery

NOTES ON THE WORKS

PLATE I. – THE MADONNA DELLA VITTORIA.
(In the Louvre)

This beautiful composition, considered one of Mantegna's greatest masterpieces, was painted in 1495-96 in commemoration of the victory won at Fornovo on July 6, 1494, by the Marquis of Mantua as generalissimo of the united Italian forces. It is now in the Louvre, Paris, having been carried off by the French in 1797.

PLATE II. – THE ADORATION OF THE KINGS
(In the Uffizi Gallery, Florence)

The central composition of a triptych, now in the Uffizi Gallery, Florence, belonging to Mantegna's second period of art development. Supposed to have been painted for the chapel of the Castello at Mantua about 1464.

PLATE III. – PORTRAIT OF A MEMBER OF THE GONZAGA FAMILY
(In the Pitti Palace, Florence)

This fine portrait, now in the Pitti Palace, Florence, represents one of the members of the Gonzaga family who were introduced in the famous frescoes by Mantegna that adorned the Camera degli Sposi and other apartments in the Castello of Mantua.

PLATE IV. – THE AGONY IN THE GARDEN
(In the National Gallery)

This beautiful composition, now in the National Gallery, London, is supposed to be a replica of the "Mount of Olives" that originally formed part of the predella of the great altar-piece of San Zeno, Verona, and to have been painted in 1439 for Giacomo Antonio Marcello, then Podestà of Padua.

PLATE V. – THE MADONNA AND CHILD SURROUNDED BY CHERUBS
(In the Brera Gallery, Milan)

This charming composition, now in the Brera Gallery, Milan, was painted in 1485 for the young Marquis of Mantua, Gian Francesco Gonzaga, as a gift for the Duchess Eleanora of Ferrara, mother of his affianced bride, Isabella d'Este. It is considered one of the finest of Mantegna's later religious pictures.

PLATE VI. – THE MADONNA AND CHILD OF THE GROTTO
(In the Uffizi Gallery, Florence)

This severe and dignified group, now in the Uffizi Gallery, Florence, is supposed by some critics to have been painted in Mantua about the same time as the frescoes of the Camera degli Sposi, whilst others assign it to a much later date, declaring it to have been produced between 1488-1490 during the artist's residence in Rome.

PLATE VII. – PARNASSUS
(In the Louvre)

This charmingly dramatic interpretation of the subjugation of the God of War by the Goddess of Love is one of a series of allegorical pictures painted for the "Studio" of the Marchesa Isabella Gonzaga at Mantua, and is a unique example of its artist's deep sympathy with the spirit of classic legend.

PLATE VIII. – THE TRIUMPH OF SCIPIO
(In the National Gallery)

Painted in 1506, this fine decorative picture in monochrome, now in the National Gallery, is one of Mantegna's latest works, and represents two incidents of the second Punic War – the arrival at Rome of the image of the goddess Cybele, and the supposed miracle wrought by it.

On the following pages are some illustrations of contemporaries of Andreas Mantegna.

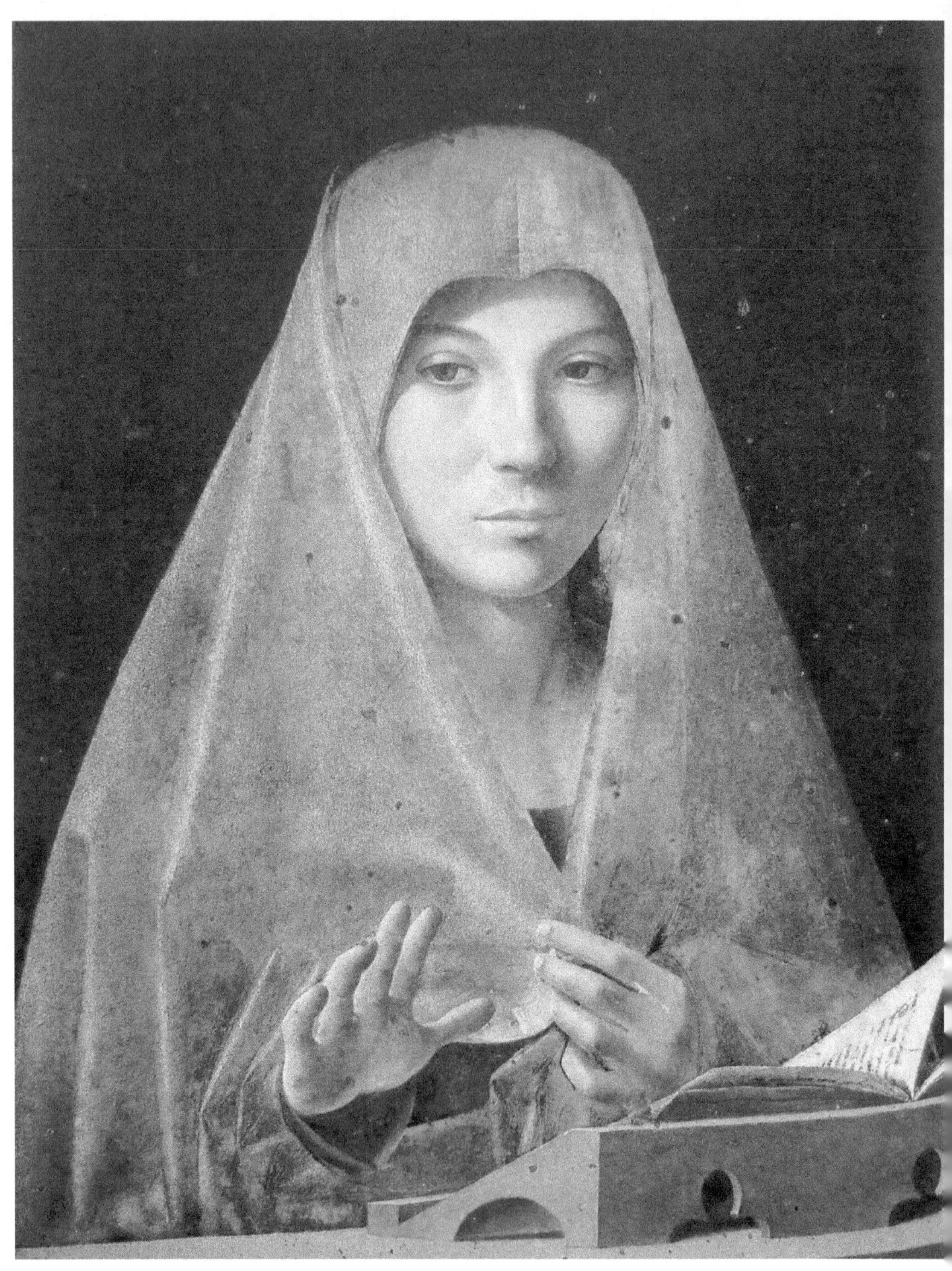

Antonello da Messina, The Virgin of the Annunciation, 1475, Palermo

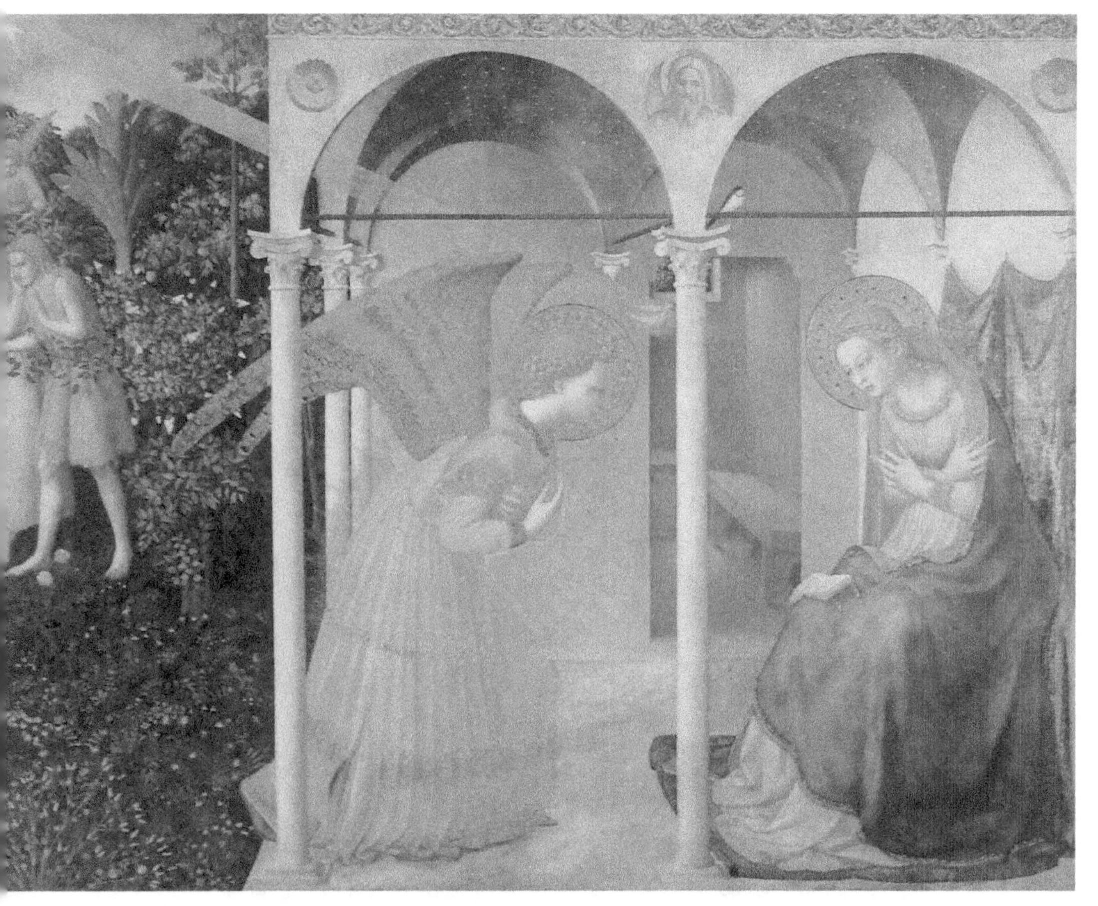

Fra Angelico, Annunciation, Prado, Madrid

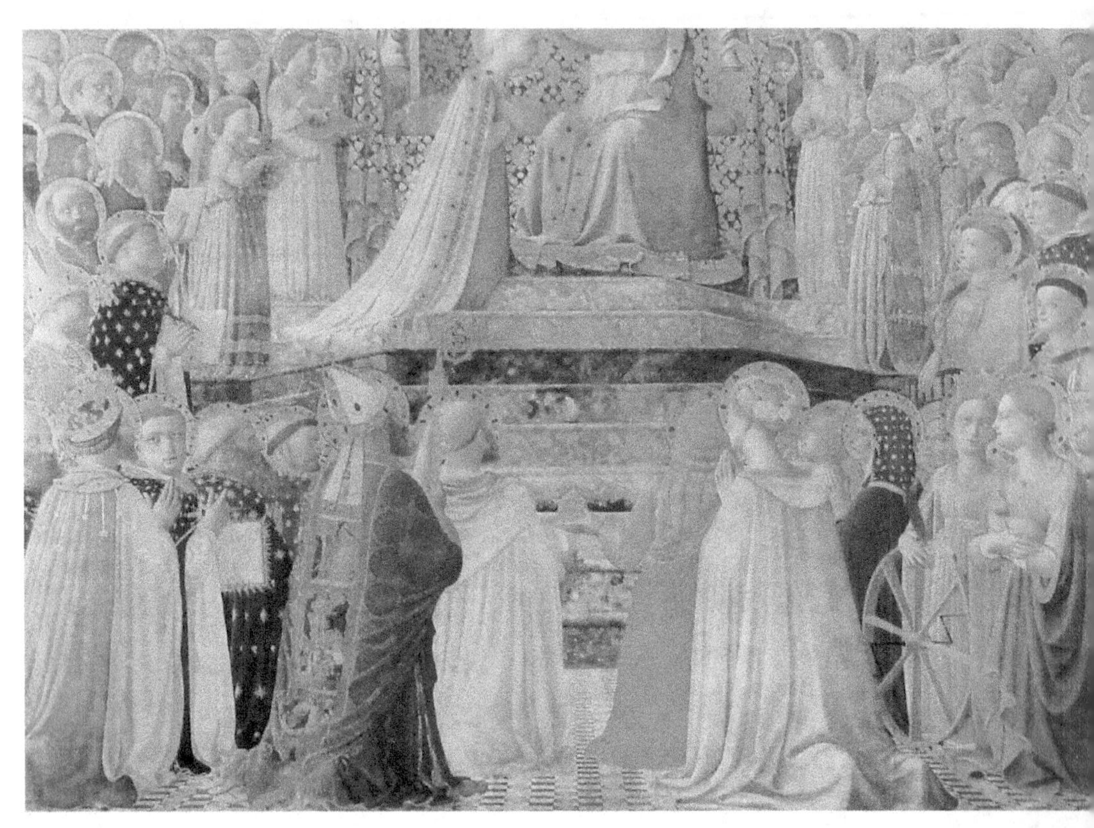

Fra Angelico, The Coronation of the Virgin, Louve, Paris, detail

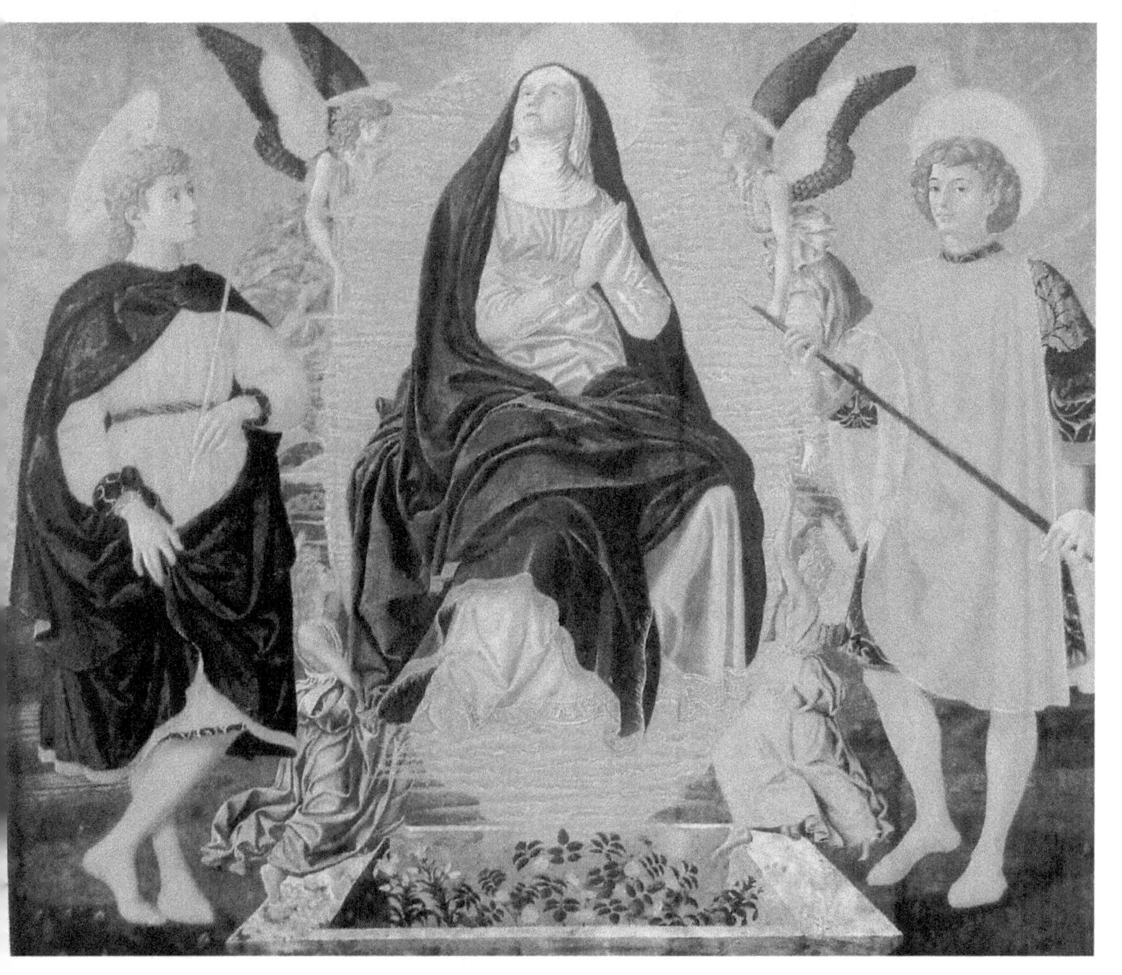

Andrea del Castagno, Assumption, Berlin

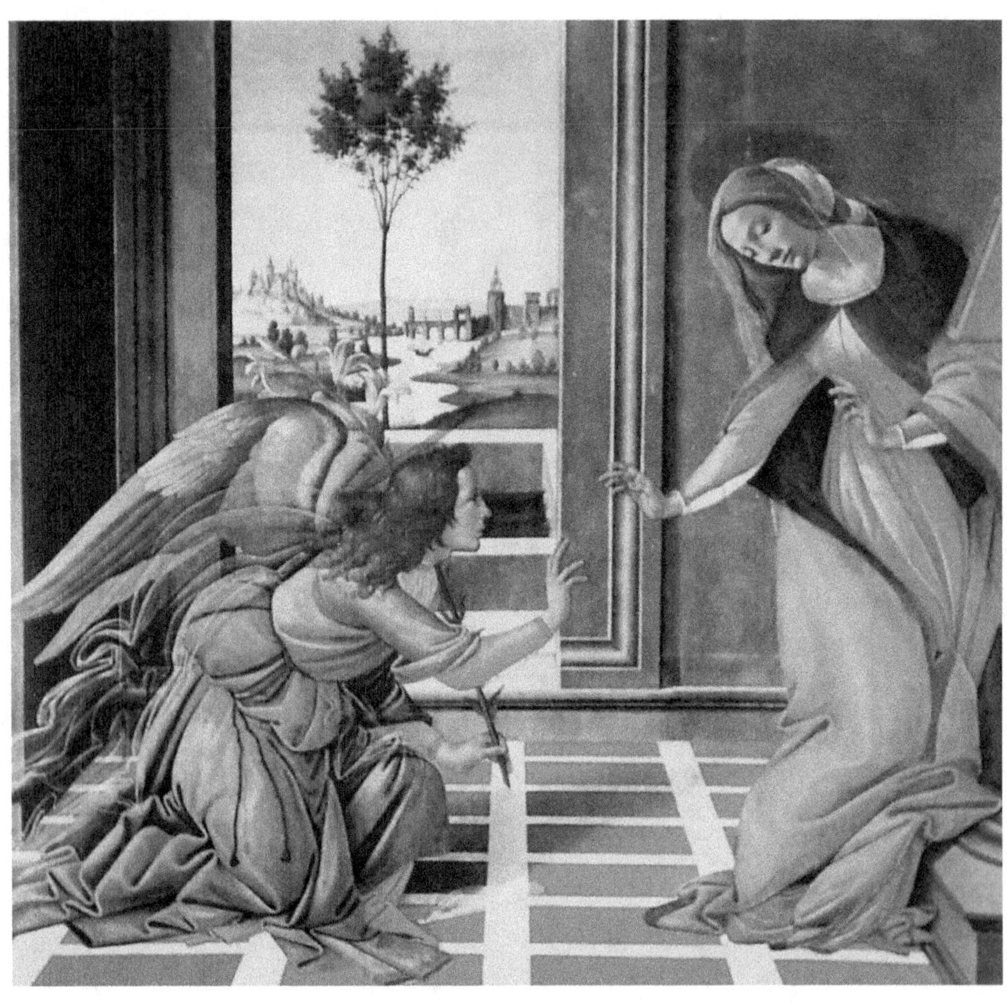

Sandro Botticelli, The Annunciation, Uffizi Gallery, Florence

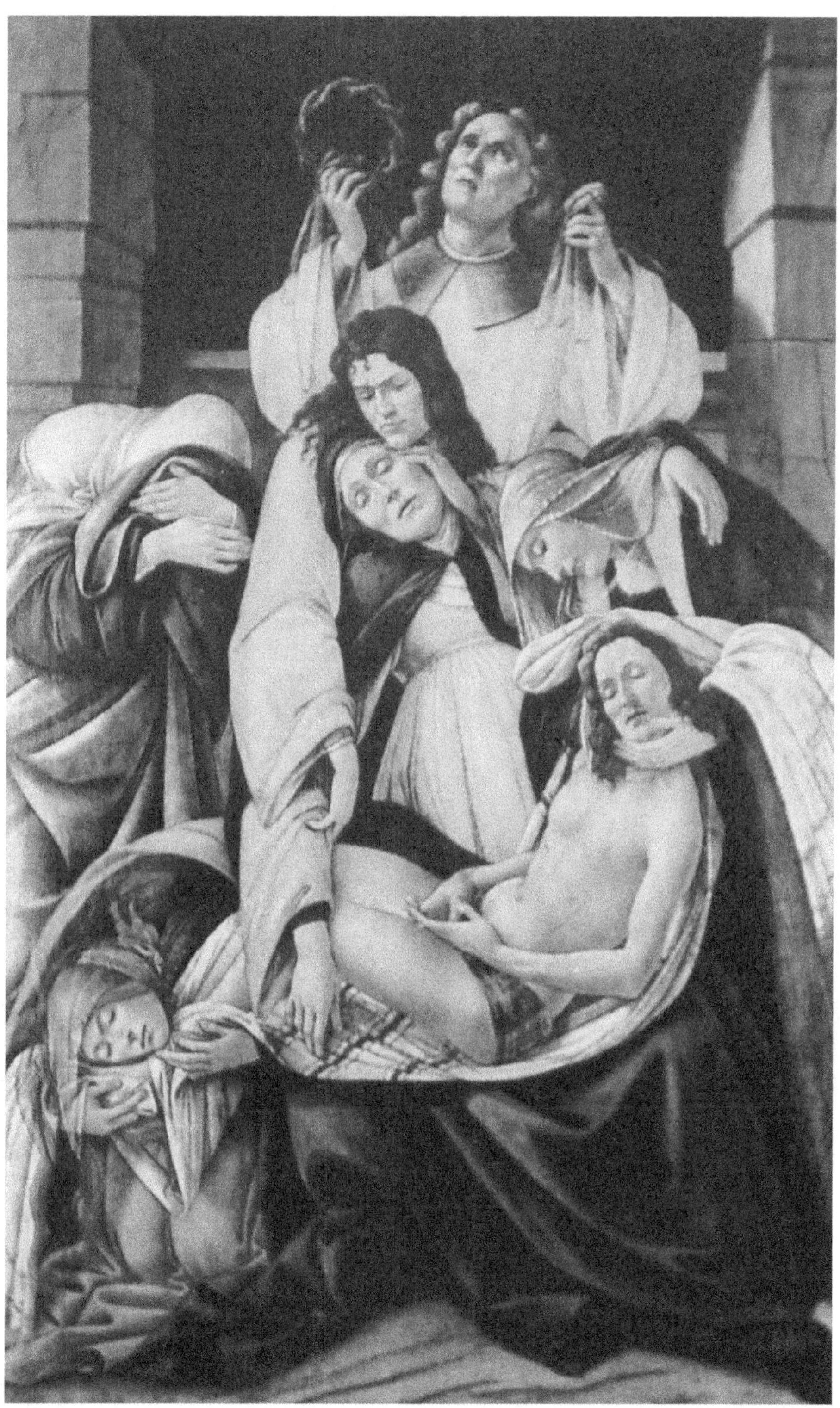

Sandro Botticelli, Pietà, Milan

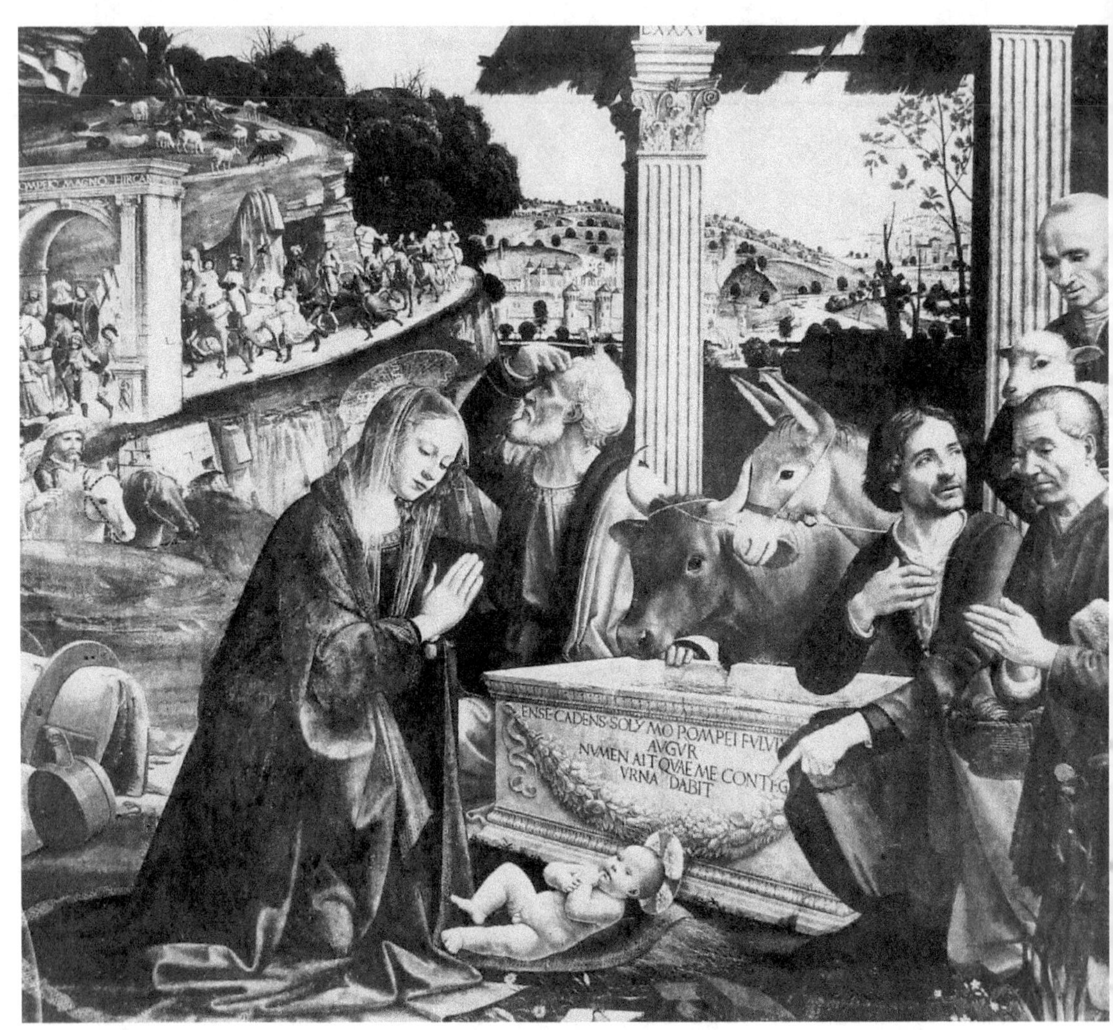

Domenico Ghirlandaio, Adoration of the Shepherds, 1485

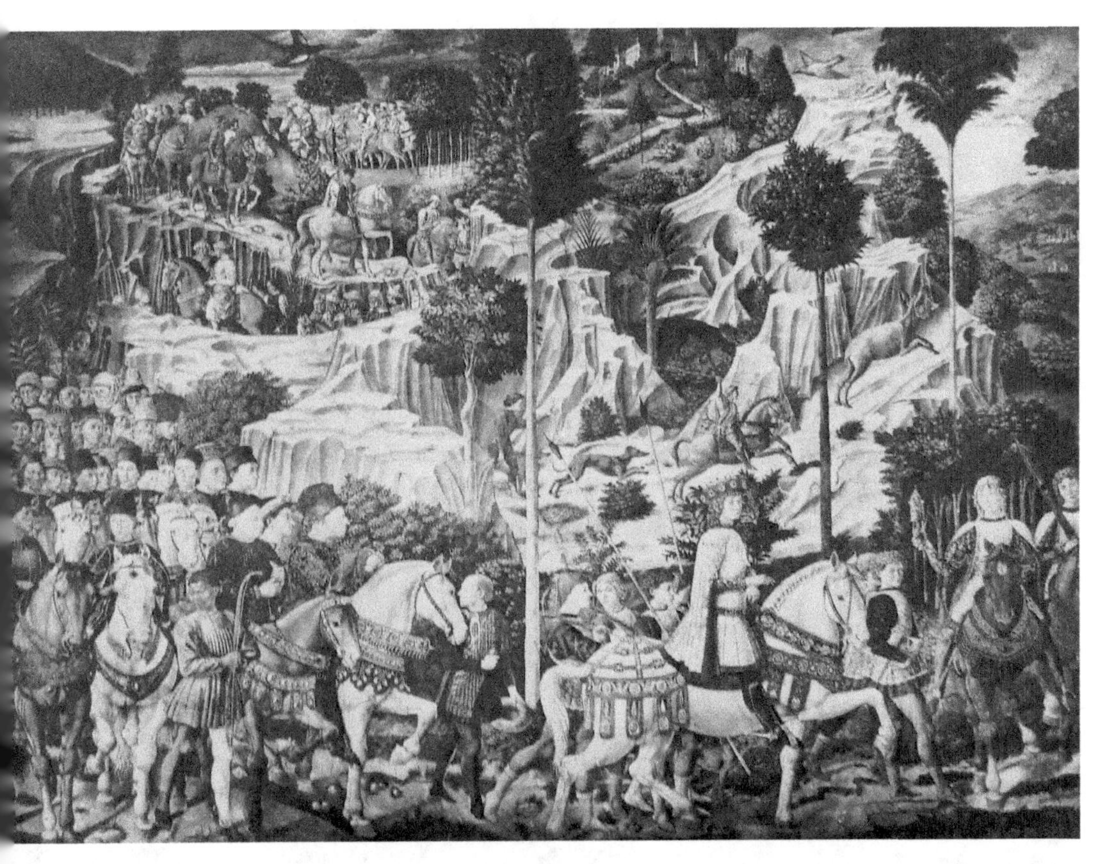

Benozzo Gozzoli, Journey of the Magi

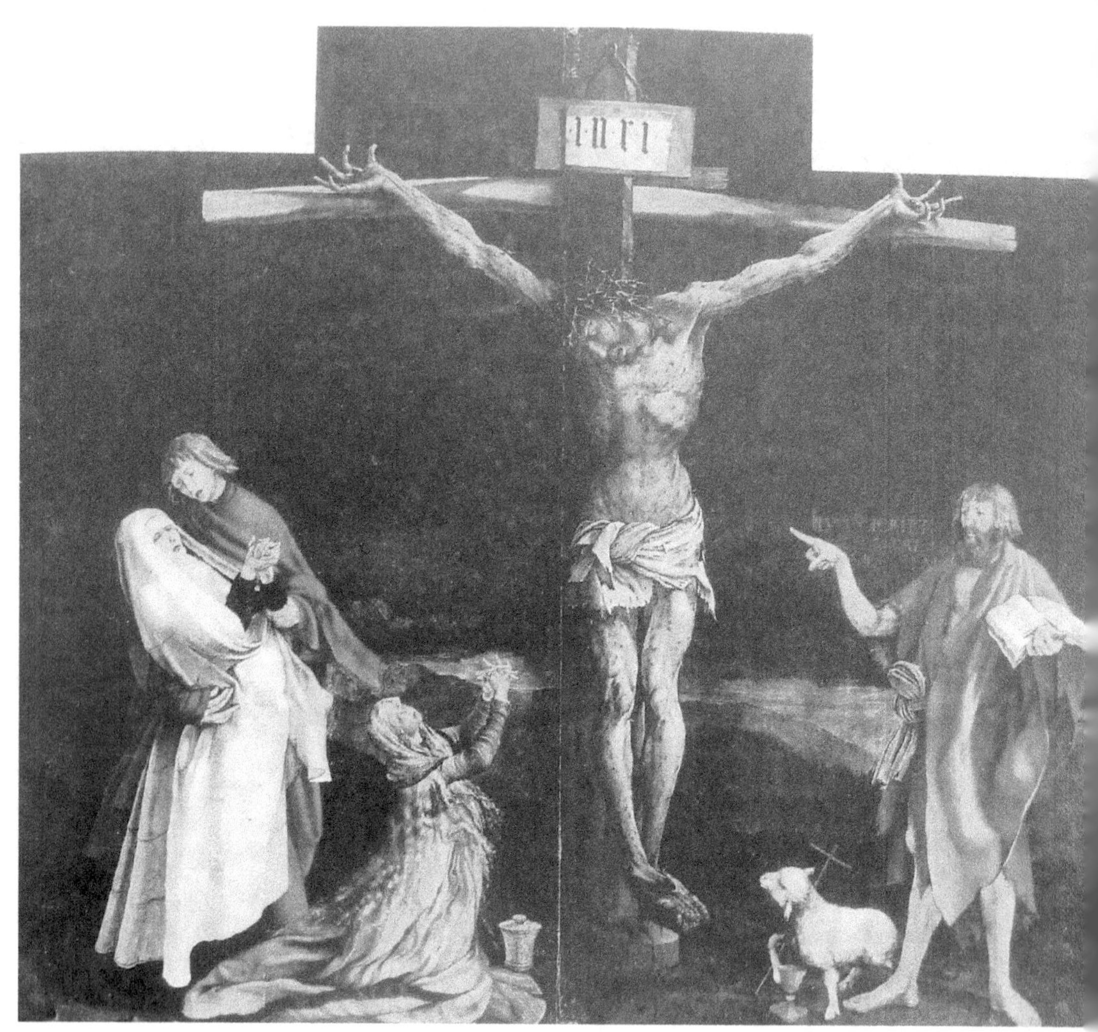

Matthias Grünewald, Crucifixion, Isenheim Altarpiece

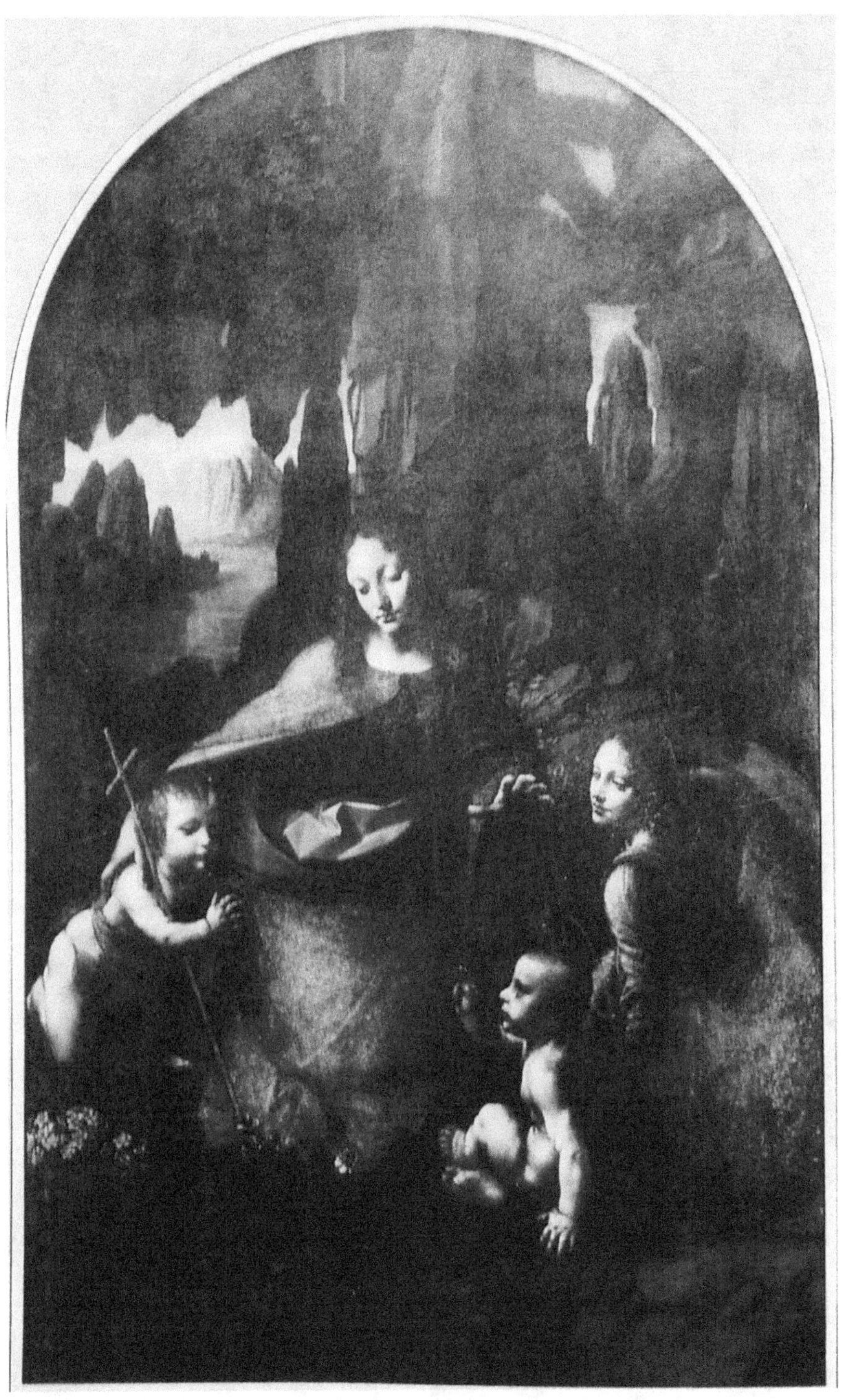

Leonardo da Vinci, The Madonna of the Rocks, London

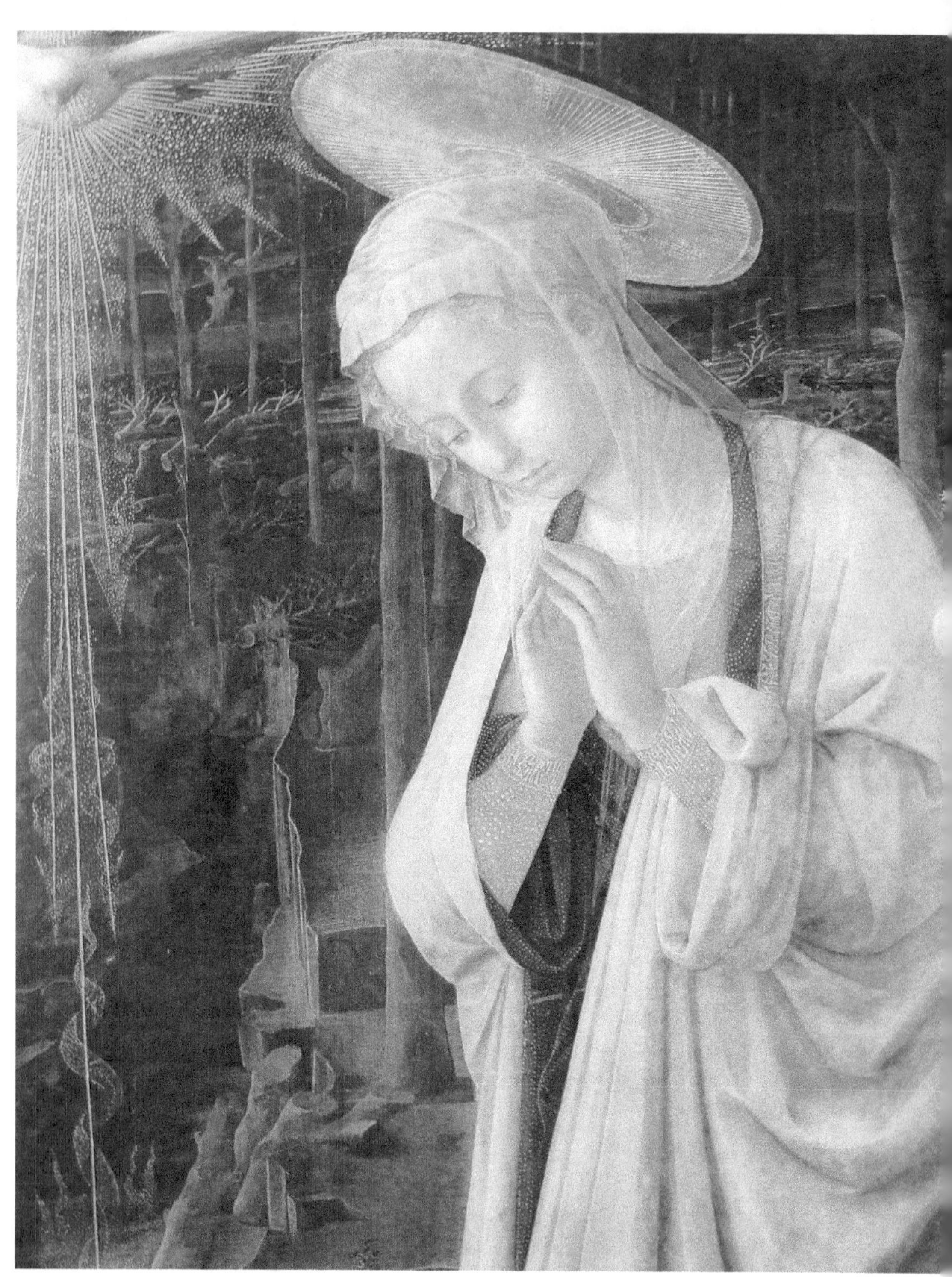

Fra Filippo Lippi, The Adoration of the Virgin, Berlin, detail

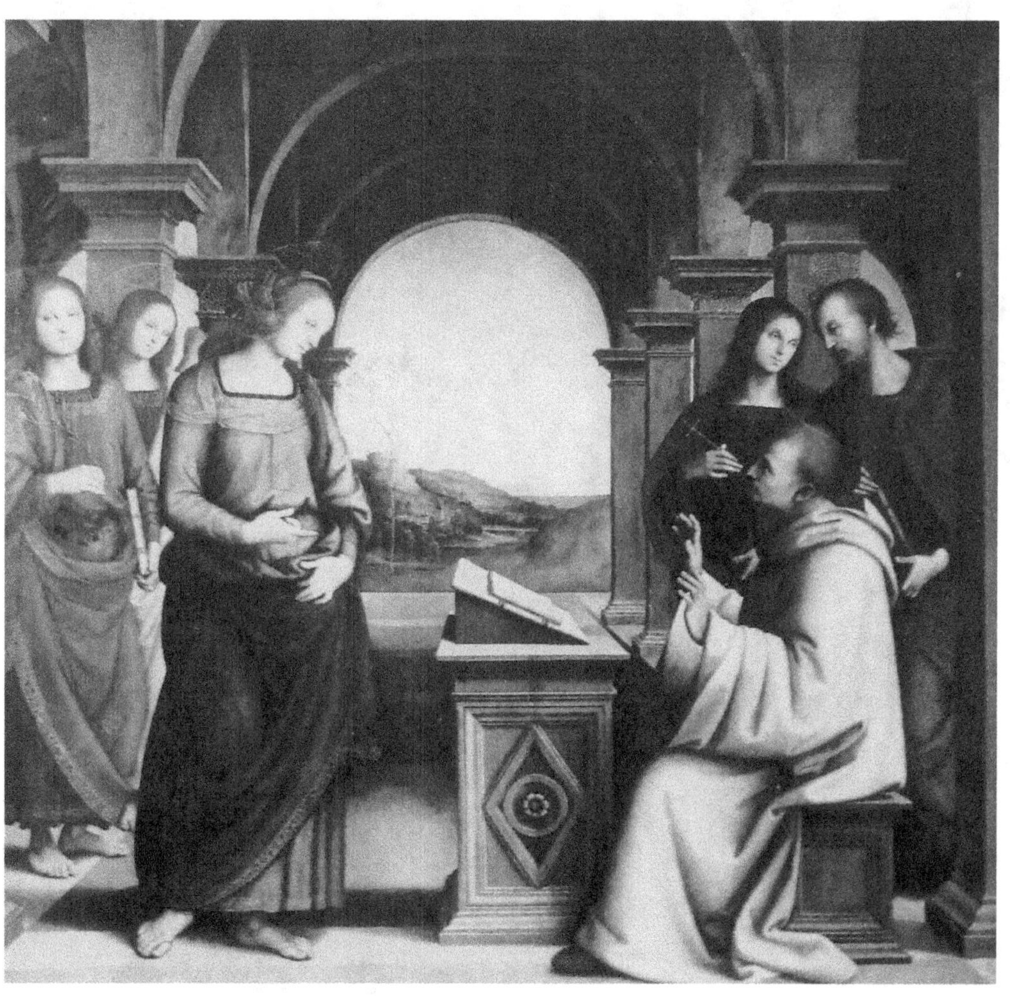

Perugino, Vision of St Bernard, 1488

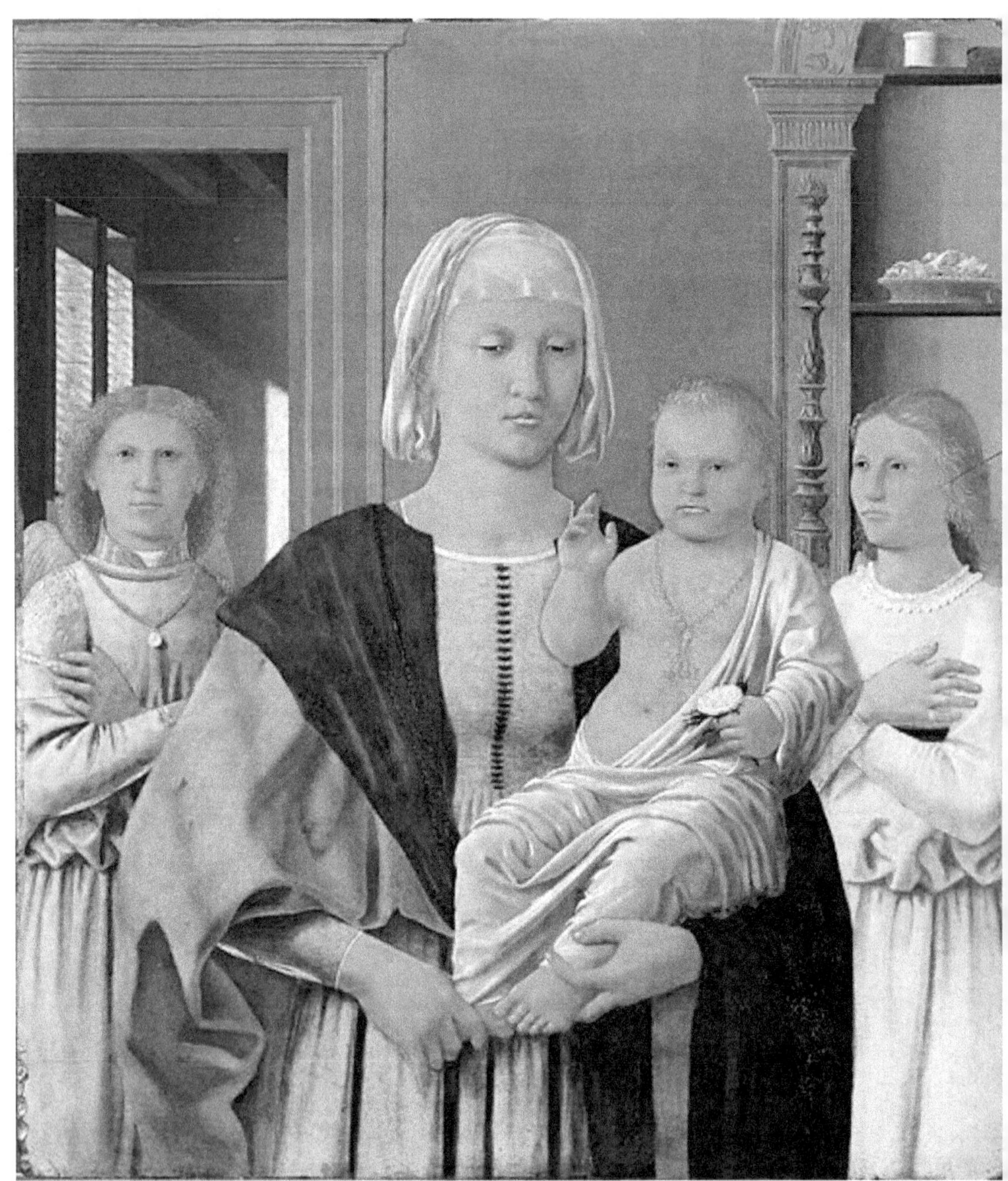

Piero della Francesca, The Brera Madonna

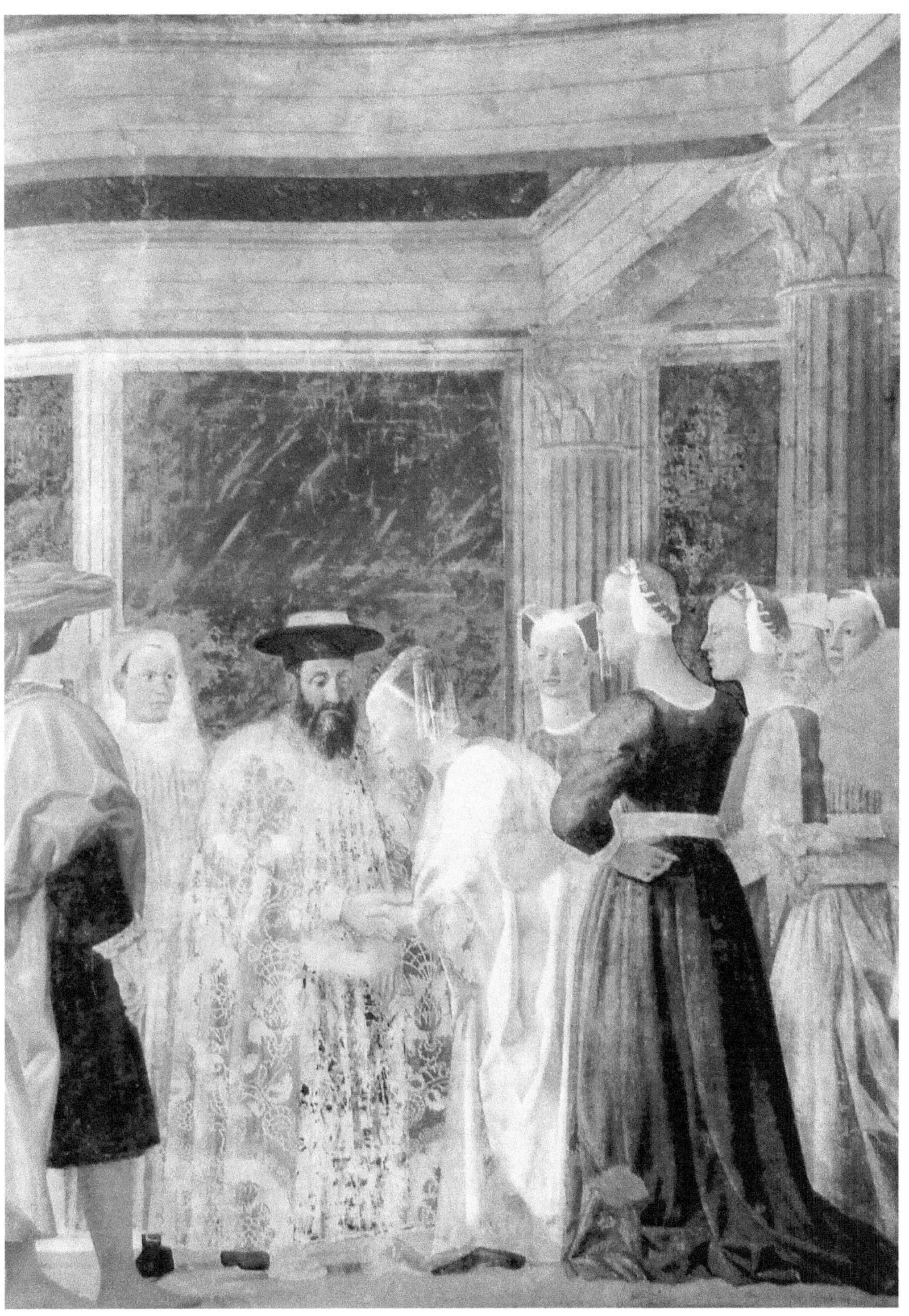

Piero della Francesca, frescoes, Arezzo

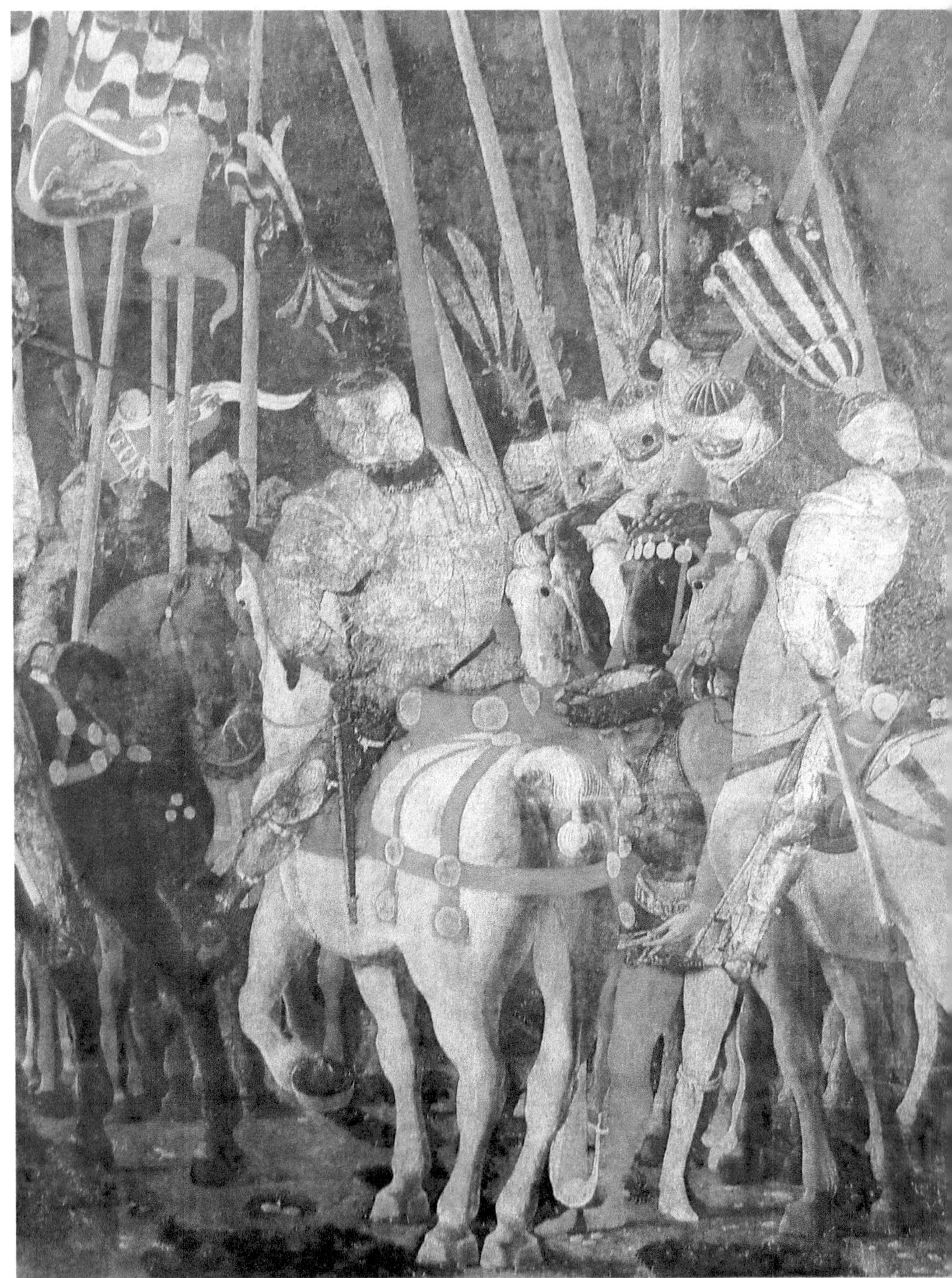

Paolo Uccello, The Battle of San Romano, Paris

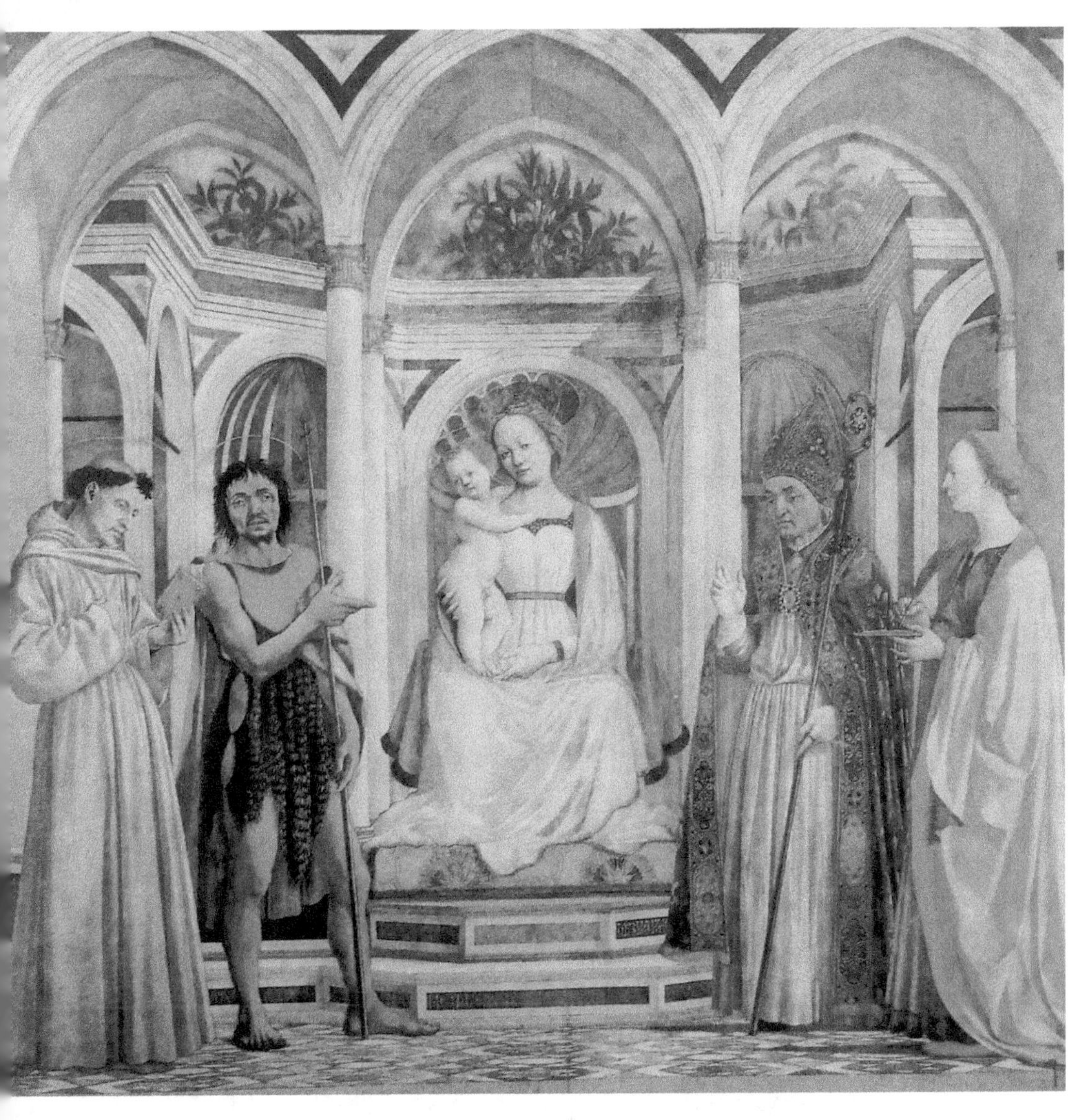

Domenico Veneziano, Madonna and Child With Saints, 1445, Uffizi Gallery

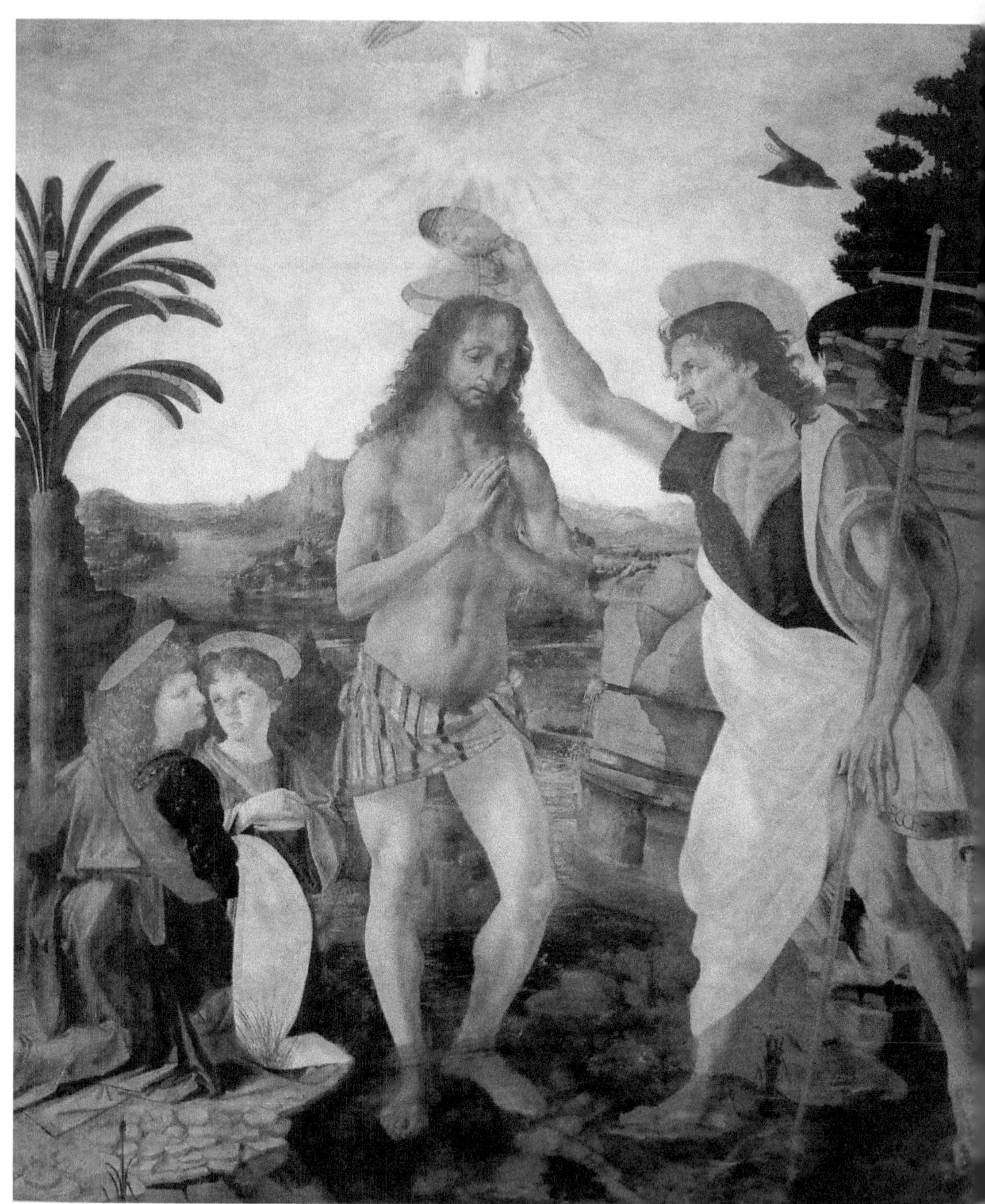

Andrea del Verrocchio, The Baptism of Christ

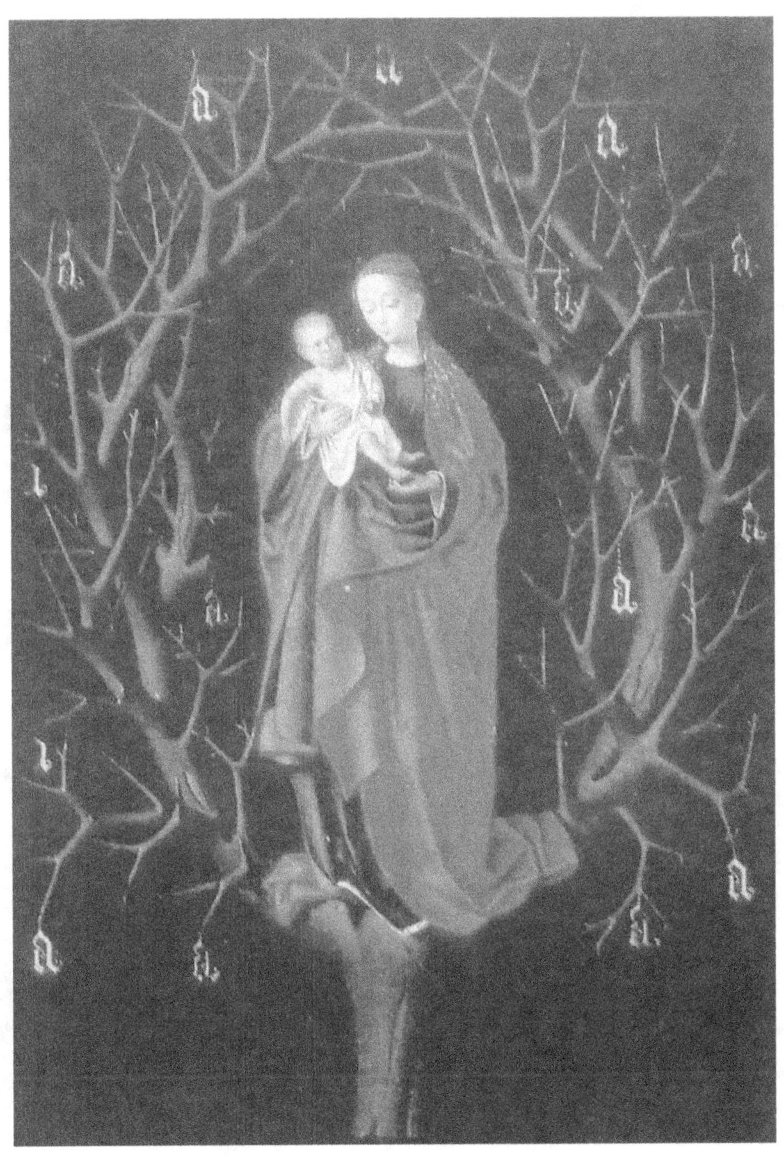

Petrus Christus, Madonna In a Barren Tree, 1450,
Prado, Madrid

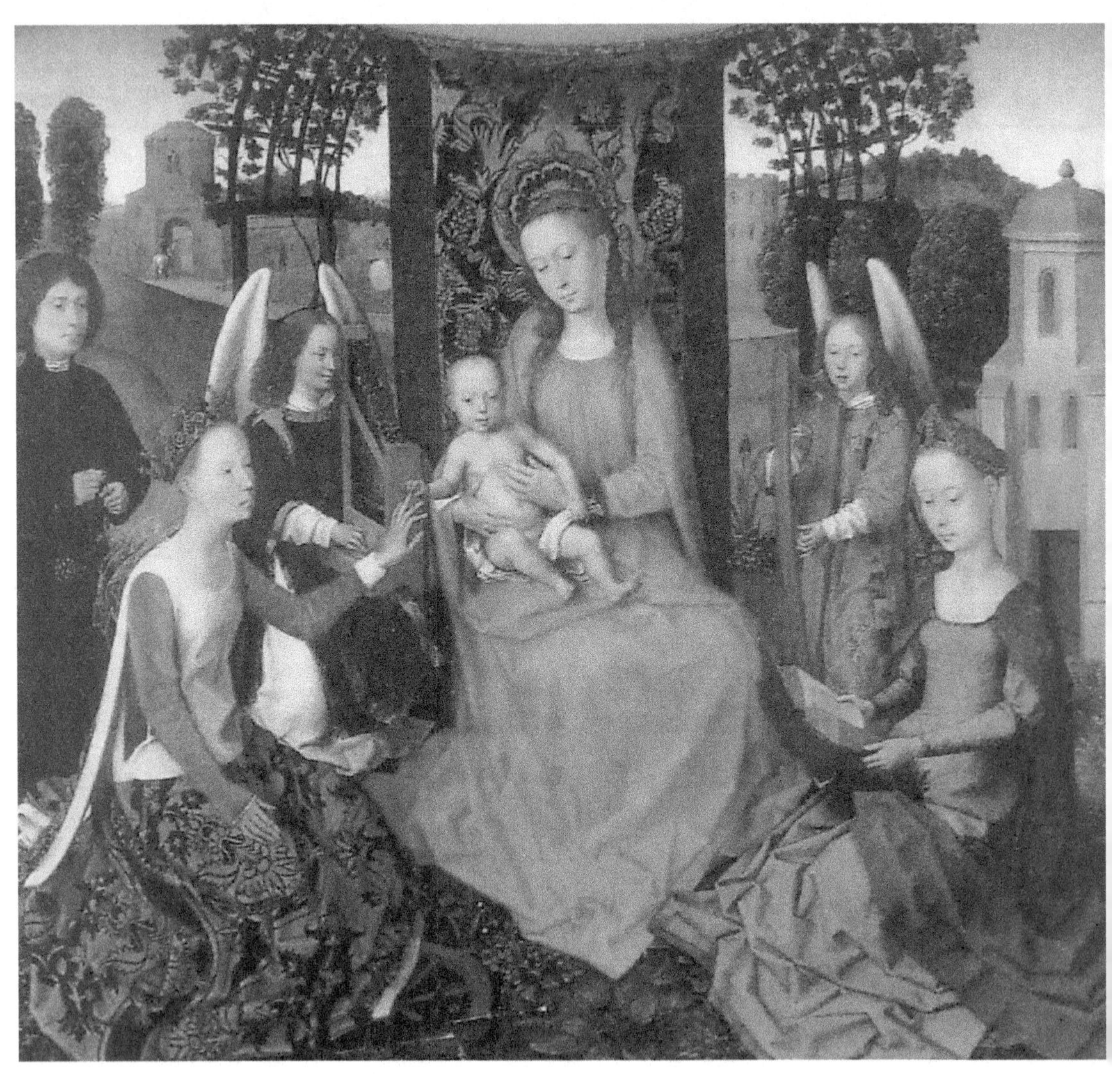

Hans Memling, The Mystic Marriage of St Catherine, Metropolitan
Museum, New York City

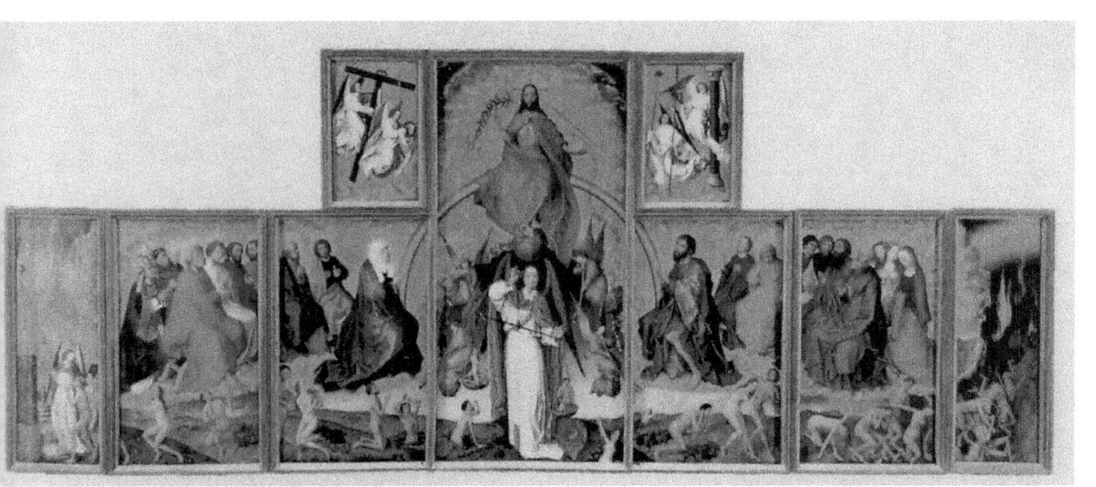

Rogier van der Weyden, The Last Judgement, 1445-49, Beaune

MAURICE SENDAK
& the art of children's book illustration

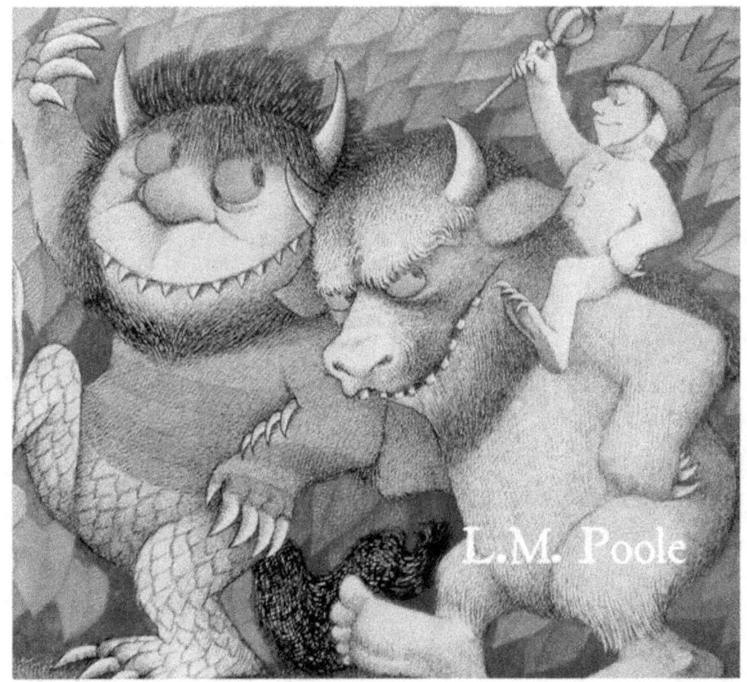

Maurice Sendak is the widely acclaimed American children's book author and illustrator. This critical study focuses on his famous trilogy, *Where the Wild Things Are, In the Night Kitchen* and *Outside Over There*, as well as the early works and Sendak's superb depictions of the Grimm Brothers' fairy tales in *The Juniper Tree*. L.M. Poole begins with a chapter on children's book illustration, in particular the treatment of fairy tales. Sendak's work is situated within the history of children's book illustration, and he is compared with many contemporary authors.

Fully illustrated. The book has been revised and updated for this edition.
ISBN 9781861714282 Pbk   ISBN 9781861713469 Hbk

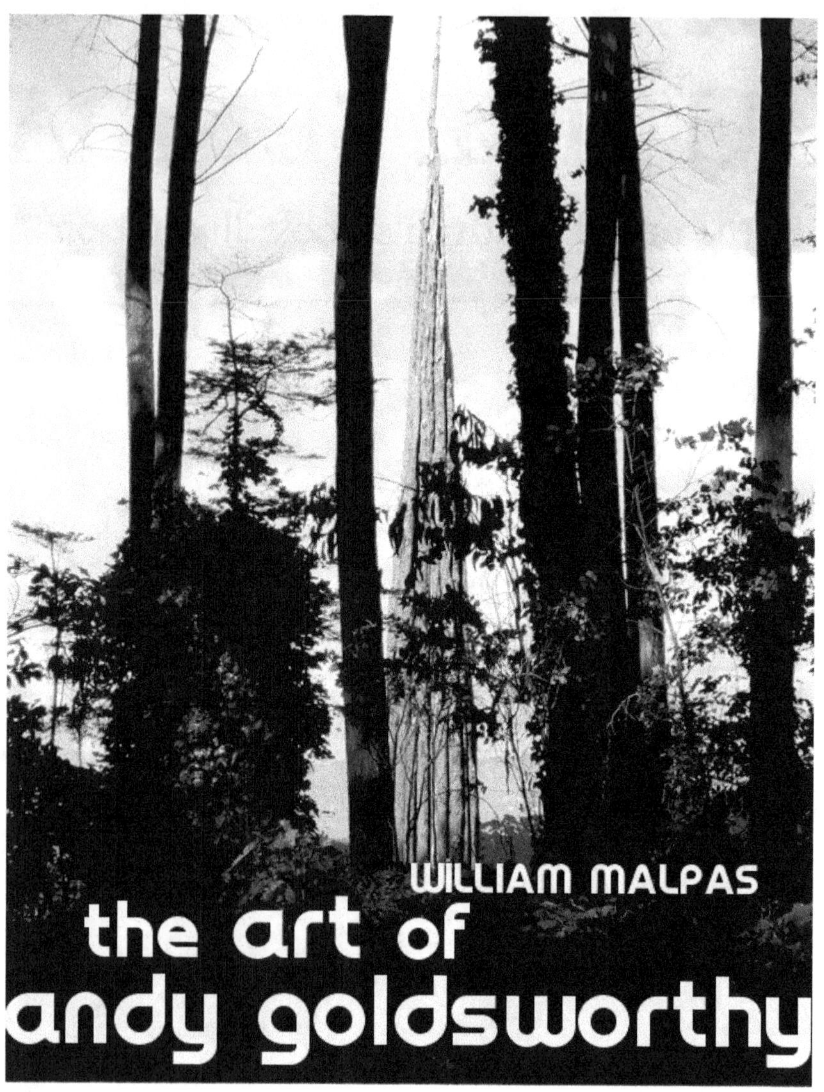

This is the most comprehensive and detailed account of the art of Andy Goldsworthy available.

This study of Andy Goldsworthy discusses all of Goldsworthy's major exhibitions, books and projects, including the *Sheepfolds* project; *Garden of Stones* in New York; TV and dance collaborations; and the books *Wood, Stone, Time* and *Passage*. William Malpas surveys all of Goldsworthy's output, and analyzes his relation with other land artists such as Robert Smithson, the Christos, Walter de Maria, Chris Drury, Richard Long and David Nash; women sculptors; sculpture in the modern era; and Goldsworthy's place in the contemporary British art scene.

The book has been updated and revised for this new edition.

ISBN 9781861714107 Pbk   ISBN 9781861714114 Hbk
Fully illustrated   www.crmoon.com

CRESCENT MOON PUBLISHING

web: www.crmoon.com e-mail: cresmopub@yahoo.co.uk

ARTS, PAINTING, SCULPTURE

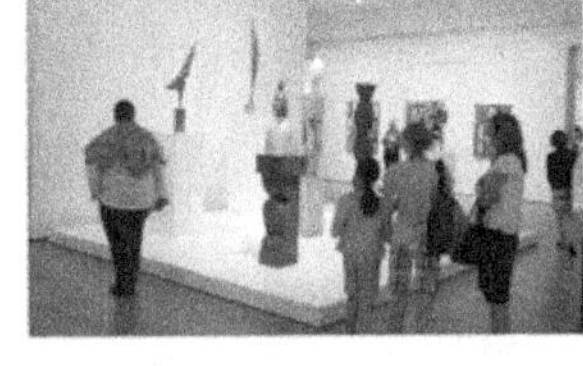
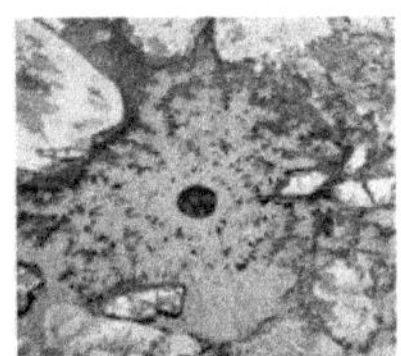
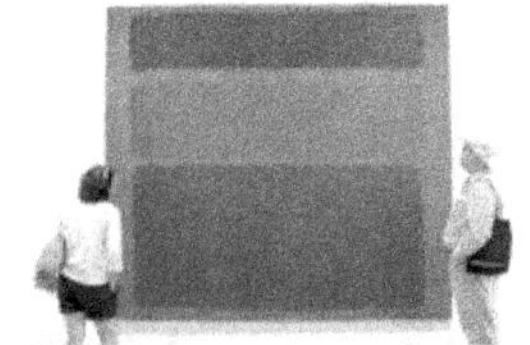

The Art of Andy Goldsworthy
Andy Goldsworthy: Touching Nature
Andy Goldsworthy in Close-Up
Andy Goldsworthy: Pocket Guide
Andy Goldsworthy In America
Land Art: A Complete Guide
The Art of Richard Long
Richard Long: Pocket Guide
Land Art In the UK
Land Art in Close-Up
Land Art In the U.S.A.
Land Art: Pocket Guide
Installation Art in Close-Up
Minimal Art and Artists In the 1960s and After
Colourfield Painting
Land Art DVD, TV documentary
Andy Goldsworthy DVD, TV documentary
The Erotic Object: Sexuality in Sculpture From Prehistory to the Present Day
Sex in Art: Pornography and Pleasure in Painting and Sculpture
Postwar Art
Sacred Gardens: The Garden in Myth, Religion and Art
Glorification: Religious Abstraction in Renaissance and 20th Century Art
Early Netherlandish Painting
Leonardo da Vinci
Piero della Francesca
Giovanni Bellini
Fra Angelico: Art and Religion in the Renaissance
Mark Rothko: The Art of Transcendence
Frank Stella: American Abstract Artist
Jasper Johns
Brice Marden
Alison Wilding: The Embrace of Sculpture
Vincent van Gogh: Visionary Landscapes
Eric Gill: Nuptials of God
Constantin Brancusi: Sculpting the Essence of Things
Max Beckmann
Caravaggio
Gustave Moreau
Egon Schiele: Sex and Death In Purple Stockings
Delizioso Fotografico Fervore: Works In Process 1
Sacro Cuore: Works In Process 2
The Light Eternal: J.M.W. Turner
The Madonna Glorified: Karen Arthurs

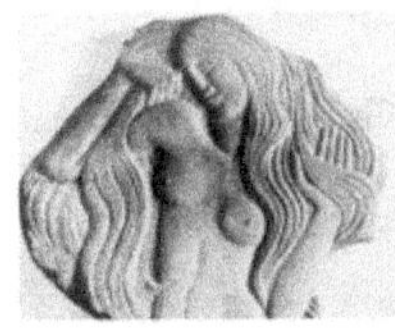
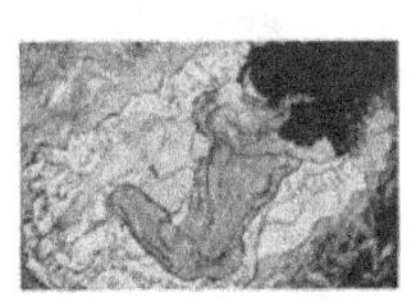
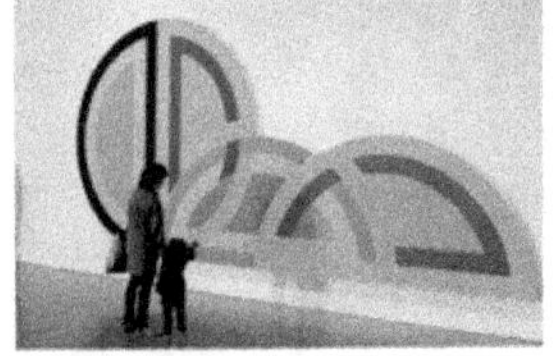
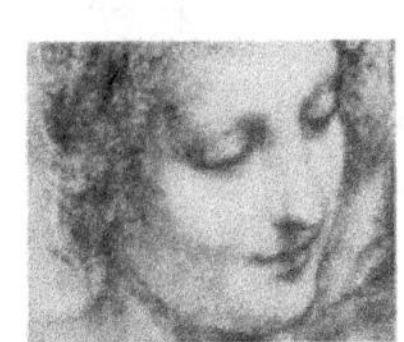
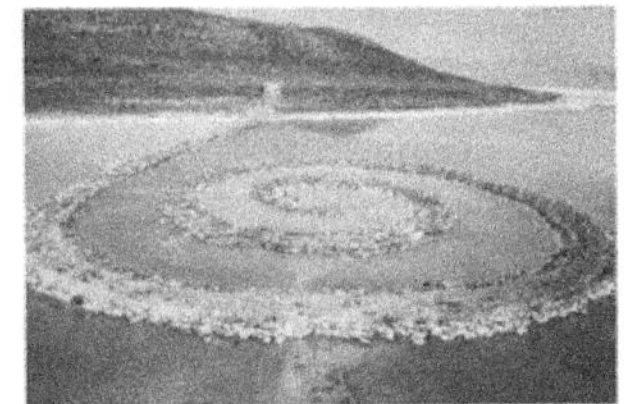

LITERATURE

J.R.R. Tolkien: The Books, The Films, The Whole Cultural Phenomenon
J.R.R. Tolkien: Pocket Guide
Tolkien's Heroic Quest
The *Earthsea* Books of Ursula Le Guin
Beauties, Beasts and Enchantment: Classic French Fairy Tales
German Popular Stories by the Brothers Grimm
Philip Pullman and *His Dark Materials*
Sexing Hardy: Thomas Hardy and Feminism
Thomas Hardy's *Tess of the d'Urbervilles*
Thomas Hardy's *Jude the Obscure*
Thomas Hardy: The Tragic Novels
Love and Tragedy: Thomas Hardy
The Poetry of Landscape in Hardy
Wessex Revisited: Thomas Hardy and John Cowper Powys
Wolfgang Iser: Essays and Interviews
Petrarch, Dante and the Troubadours
Maurice Sendak and the Art of Children's Book Illustration
Andrea Dworkin
Cixous, Irigaray, Kristeva: The *Jouissance* of French Feminism
Julia Kristeva: Art, Love, Melancholy, Philosophy, Semiotics and Psychoanalysis
Hélene Cixous I Love You: The *Jouissance* of Writing
Luce Irigaray: Lips, Kissing, and the Politics of Sexual Difference
Peter Redgrove: Here Comes the Flood
Peter Redgrove: Sex-Magic-Poetry-Cornwall
Lawrence Durrell: Between Love and Death, East and West
Love, Culture & Poetry: Lawrence Durrell
Cavafy: Anatomy of a Soul
German Romantic Poetry: Goethe, Novalis, Heine, Hölderlin
Feminism and Shakespeare
Shakespeare: Love, Poetry & Magic
The Passion of D.H. Lawrence
D.H. Lawrence: Symbolic Landscapes
D.H. Lawrence: Infinite Sensual Violence
Rimbaud: Arthur Rimbaud and the Magic of Poetry
The Ecstasies of John Cowper Powys
Sensualism and Mythology: The Wessex Novels of John Cowper Powys
Amorous Life: John Cowper Powys and the Manifestation of Affectivity (H.W. Fawkner)
Postmodern Powys: New Essays on John Cowper Powys (Joe Boulter)
Rethinking Powys: Critical Essays on John Cowper Powys
Paul Bowles & Bernardo Bertolucci
Rainer Maria Rilke
Joseph Conrad: *Heart of Darkness*
In the Dim Void: Samuel Beckett
Samuel Beckett Goes into the Silence
André Gide: Fiction and Fervour
Jackie Collins and the Blockbuster Novel
Blinded By Her Light: The Love-Poetry of Robert Graves
The Passion of Colours: Travels In Mediterranean Lands
Poetic Forms

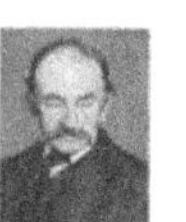
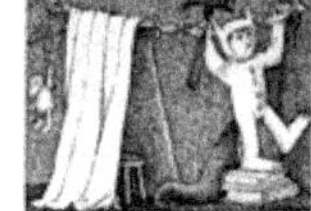
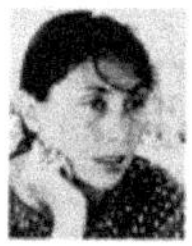
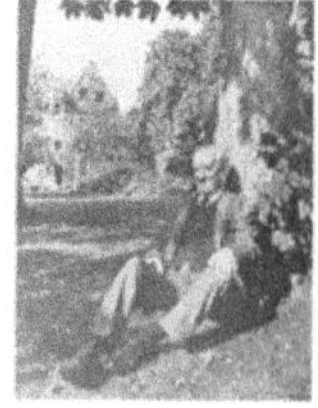
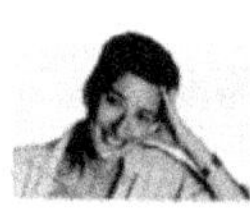
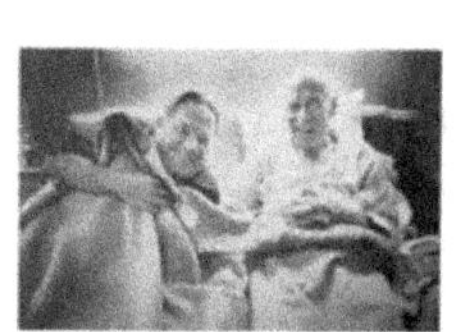
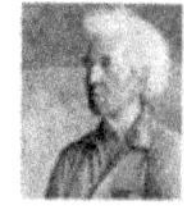
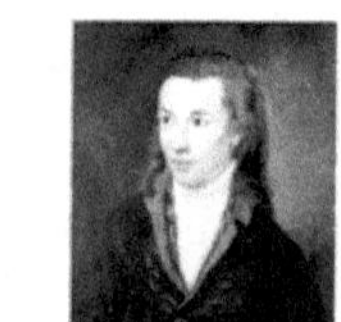

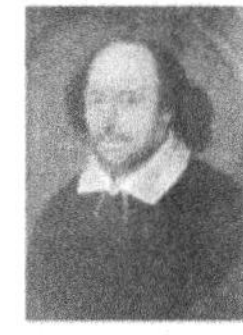
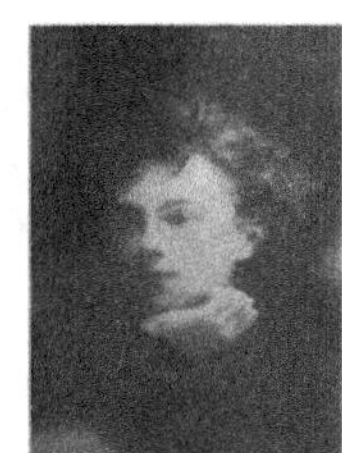
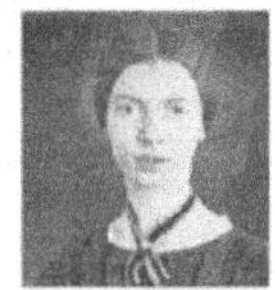
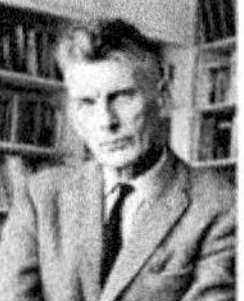
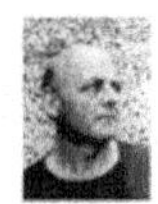
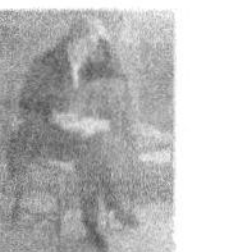
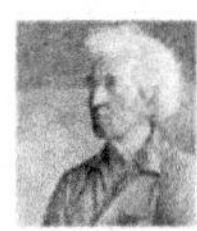
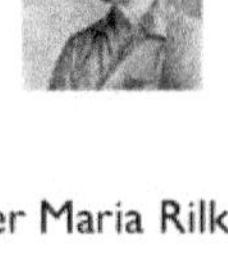
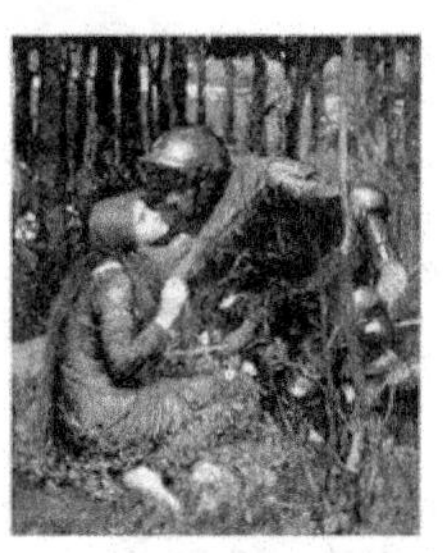
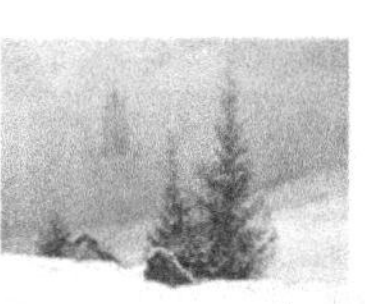
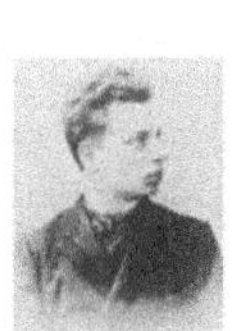
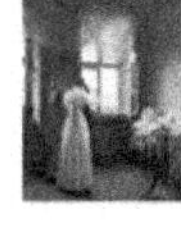

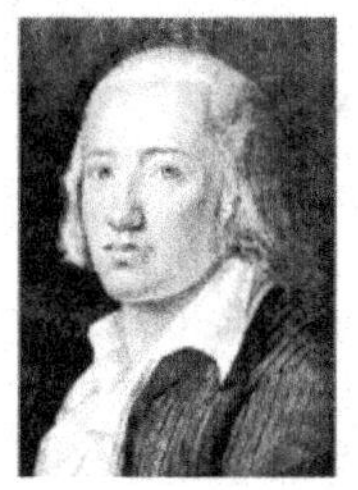
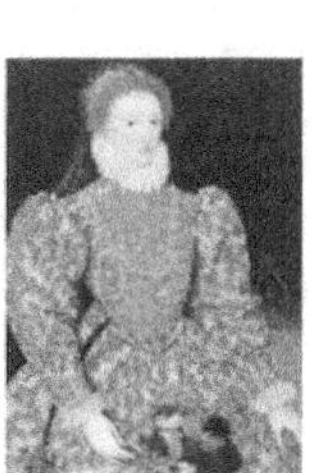

MEDIA, CINEMA, FEMINISM and CULTURAL STUDIES

J.R.R. Tolkien: The Books, The Films, The Whole Cultural Phenomenon
J.R.R. Tolkien: Pocket Guide
The *Lord of the Rings* Movies: Pocket Guide
The Cinema of Hayao Miyazaki
Hayao Miyazaki: *Princess Mononoke*: Pocket Movie Guide
Hayao Miyazaki: *Spirited Away*: Pocket Movie Guide
Tim Burton : Hallowe'en For Hollywood
Ken Russell
Ken Russell: *Tommy*: Pocket Movie Guide
The Ghost Dance: The Origins of Religion
The Peyote Cult
Cixous, Irigaray, Kristeva: The *Jouissance* of French Feminism
Julia Kristeva: Art, Love, Melancholy, Philosophy, Semiotics and Psychoanalysis
Luce Irigaray: Lips, Kissing, and the Politics of Sexual Difference
Hélene Cixous I Love You: The *Jouissance* of Writing
Andrea Dworkin
'Cosmo Woman': The World of Women's Magazines
Women in Pop Music
HomeGround: The Kate Bush Anthology
Discovering the Goddess (Geoffrey Ashe)
The Poetry of Cinema
The Sacred Cinema of Andrei Tarkovsky
Andrei Tarkovsky: Pocket Guide
Andrei Tarkovsky: *Mirror*: Pocket Movie Guide
Andrei Tarkovsky: *The Sacrifice*: Pocket Movie Guide
Walerian Borowczyk: Cinema of Erotic Dreams
Jean-Luc Godard: The Passion of Cinema
Jean-Luc Godard: *Hail Mary*: Pocket Movie Guide
Jean-Luc Godard: *Contempt*: Pocket Movie Guide
Jean-Luc Godard: *Pierrot le Fou*: Pocket Movie Guide
John Hughes and Eighties Cinema
Ferris Bueller's Day Off: Pocket Movie Guide
Jean-Luc Godard: Pocket Guide
The Cinema of Richard Linklater
Liv Tyler: Star In Ascendance
Blade Runner and the Films of Philip K. Dick
Paul Bowles and Bernardo Bertolucci
Media Hell: Radio, TV and the Press
An Open Letter to the BBC
Detonation Britain: Nuclear War in the UK
Feminism and Shakespeare
Wild Zones: Pornography, Art and Feminism
Sex in Art: Pornography and Pleasure in Painting and Sculpture
Sexing Hardy: Thomas Hardy and Feminism

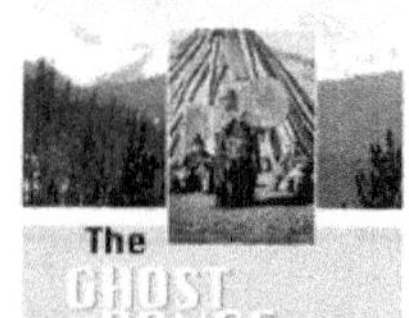
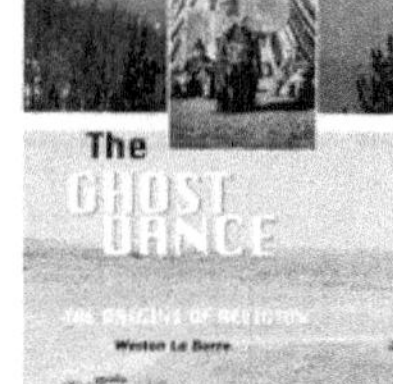
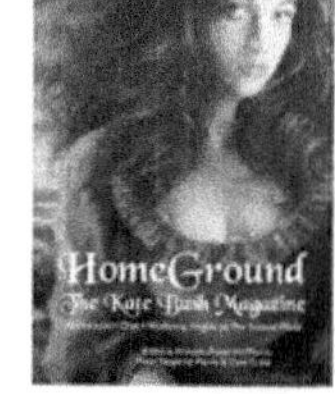
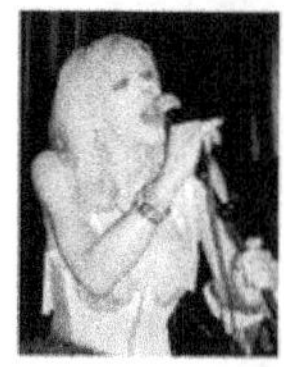
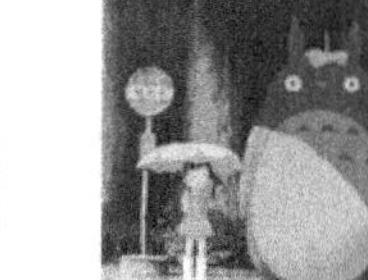
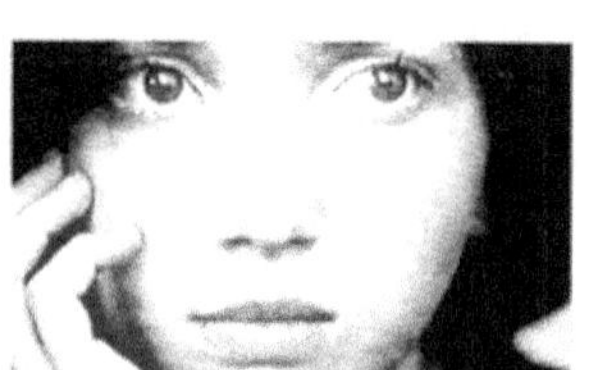

The Light Eternal is a model monograph, an exemplary job. The subject matter of the book is beautifully organised and dead on beam. (Lawrence Durrell)
It is amazing for me to see my work treated with such passion and respect. (Andrea Dworkin)

CRESCENT MOON PUBLISHING
P.O. Box 1312, Maidstone, Kent, ME14 5XU, Great Britain. www.crmoon.com

cresmopub@yahoo.co.uk   www.crescentmoon.org.uk
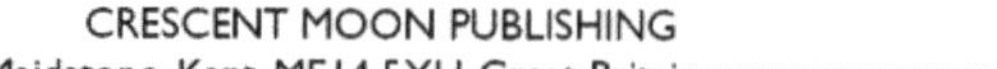